ENSEMBLE ATELIER WW
MAX DUDLER

jovis

Impressum
Imprint

© 2015 by jovis Verlag GmbH

Herausgeber und Redaktion / Editors and project management
Alexander Bonte, J. Christoph Bürkle

Lektorat / Copy-editing
Philipp Sperrle, J. Christoph Bürkle

Übersetzung / Translation
Lynne Kolar-Thompson, Feld am See

Korrektur Englisch / English proofreading
Inez Templeton, Berlin

Gestaltung und Satz / Design and setting
T616 [veruschka götz berlin] mit Katrin Kassel und Dani Ziegan

Umschlaggestaltung / Cover design
T616 [veruschka götz berlin] mit Katrin Kassel

Lithografie / Lithography
Bild1Druck, Berlin

Druck und Bindung / Printing and binding
DZA Druckerei zu Altenburg GmbH

Bibliografische Information der Deutschen Nationalbibliothek
Die Deutsche Nationalbibliothek verzeichnet diese Publikation
in der Deutschen Nationalbibliografie; detaillierte bibliografische
Daten sind im Internet über http://dnb.d-nb.de abrufbar.

Bibliographic information published by the Deutsche Nationalbibliothek. The Deutsche Nationalbibliothek lists this publication in
the Deutsche Nationalbibliografie; detailed bibliographic data are
available on the Internet at http://dnb.d-nb.de

jovis Verlag GmbH
Kurfürstenstraße 15/16
10785 Berlin

www.jovis.de

jovis-Bücher sind weltweit im ausgewählten Buchhandel erhältlich.
Informationen zu unserem internationalen Vertrieb erhalten Sie von
Ihrem Buchhändler oder unter www.jovis.de.

jovis books are available worldwide in selected bookstores. Please
contact your nearest bookseller or visit www.jovis.de for information
concerning your local distribution.

ISBN 978-3-86859-284-9

Alexander Bonte,
J. Christoph Bürkle [Hg./Eds.]

ENSEMBLE ATELIER WW
MAX DUDLER

Hochhäuser für Zürich:
Das Ensemble am Quadro-Platz

High-rises for Zurich:
The Ensemble on Quadro Square

jovis

Inhalt

Contents

Weitblick und Vertrauen
Nachhaltige Architektur für ein Quartier der Zukunft

Grußwort von Stefan Schädle
Leiter Real Estate Management BVK

d

Das neue Hochhausensemble an der Thurgauerstrasse mit 60.000 Quadratmetern Bürofläche ist eine beinahe eigenständige Stadt im boomenden Zürich-Nord. Um ein Projekt dieser Größenordnung erfolgreich zu realisieren, braucht es neben viel Überzeugungsarbeit, Mut und Voraussicht auch eine Menge Vertrauen: Vertrauen in den Standort, Vertrauen in die Qualität des Projektes und schließlich Vertrauen in die Menschen, die an diesem Projekt beteiligt sind. Erforderlich ist insbesondere die Gewissheit, das Projekt nachhaltig wirtschaftlich nutzbar machen zu können. Wir haben schon früh an den Erfolg von Quadro geglaubt und uns entschieden dafür eingesetzt.
Bauwerke wie diese müssen sich über einen Zeitraum von Generationen bewähren. Zürich-Nord ist eine der wichtigsten Wachstumsregionen der Schweiz. Ein Gebäude an diesem Standort muss nicht nur der Stadt von heute gerecht werden, sondern auch der Stadt der Zukunft.
Die zeitlose Anmutung der Häuser und ihre städtebauliche Einfügung versprechen auch künftig genauso markant und stilbildend zu sein, wie sie es nach 15 Jahren Planungs- und Bauzeit geblieben sind. Die Architektur der Gebäude des Ensembles ist in die Zukunft gedacht. In Zeiten steigender Energiekosten hat die Architektur Vorbildcharakter. Dank einer innovativen Verknüpfung von Architektur-, Energie- und Haustechnikkonzept erreichen alle Gebäude die Minergie-Label-Auszeichnung im Grundausbau. Für die BVK handelt es sich um eine Investition in die Zukunft unserer 120.000 Versicherten.
Ein solches Leuchtturmprojekt von der Vision bis zur gelungenen Umsetzung zu begleiten, erfordert neben der technischen Kompetenz auch viel Ausdauer. Für diese Leistung gratuliere ich im Namen der BVK allen Beteiligten und danke für das gegenseitige Vertrauen.

Foresight and Trust
Sustainable Architecture for a District of the Future

Preface by Stefan Schädle
Head of Real Estate Management BVK

e

The new high-rise ensemble on Thurgauerstrasse, providing 60,000 square meters of office space, forms an almost autonomous city within the city in the booming area of Zurich-Nord. Successfully realizing a project on this scale requires a great deal of persuasion, courage, and foresight, as well as a high level of trust: trust in the location, trust in the quality of the project, and finally trust in the people who are involved in this project. In particular, there has to be a conviction that the project will have a long-term economic benefit. We have believed in the success of Quadro from very early on and have supported it wholeheartedly. Buildings such as these have to prove themselves over a period of a few generations. Zurich-Nord is one of the most important growth regions in Switzerland. A building in such a location must therefore meet not only the present requirements of the city, but also those of the future.
The timeless appearance of the buildings and their integration into the urban environment promise to be just as striking and stylistically distinctive in 100 years as they have remained after fifteen years of planning and construction time. The architecture of the ensemble of buildings is future-oriented. In times of rising energy costs, the architecture is exemplary. Owing to an innovative combination of architecture, energy, and technology concepts, the standard interior finish of all buildings has been certified with the Minergie label standard. For the BVK it is an investment into the future of our 120,000 insurants.
Accompanying such a flagship project from the initial vision to its successful realization requires great perseverance, as well as technical competence. In the name of BVK, I would like to congratulate all those involved in this achievement and to thank them for the mutual trust.

Den Wandel gestalten: Ein Ensemble als Emblem

Shaping Change: An Ensemble as an Emblem

Grußwort von Ernst Schaufelberger
Head of Asset Management Switzerland,
Central & Eastern Europe
AXA Real Estate

Preface by Ernst Schaufelberger
Head of Asset Management Switzerland,
Central & Eastern Europe
AXA Real Estate

d

e

Luftbild
Aerial photograph

Ab 1856 profitiert Oerlikon von der Lage an der neu er- öffneten Eisenbahnverbindung zwischen Zürich und dem süddeutschen Raum: Durch den Standortvorteil wächst die Region zum wichtigen Industrie- und Gewerbe- standort. Heute ist die Bahnlinie zu einer Hauptachse des öffentlichen Verkehrs geworden; die Industriehallen aber wurden inzwischen durch »Denkfabriken« ersetzt: im Quartier Leutschenbach vollzieht sich seit Ende der 1990er Jahre das größte innerstädtische Umnutzungs- vorhaben der Schweiz. Mit der neuen Glattalbahn wird nach der Ansiedlung der Messe und dem Bau des Flughafens eine weitere weitsichtige Entscheidung wirksam, von der Leutschenbach und somit auch das Hochhausensemble an der Thurgauerstrasse profitieren wird. Der Quadro-Platz, der auf halber Strecke zwischen dem Flughafen und der Finanzmeile rund um den Para- deplatz liegt, wird dadurch noch mehr im Bewusstsein der Zürcher verankert.
Die herausragenden Bedingungen des Verkehrsknoten- punktes Ecke Thurgauer-/Hagenholzstrasse wurden von den Projektentwicklern der Implenia Development AG früh ausgemacht und zusammen mit der AXA Leben AG und der BVK als Investoren mit größtmöglicher Konse- quenz entwickelt. Investoren, Projektentwickler, Archi- tekten und auch die Stadt Zürich haben auf dem Weg zum fertigen Bau etliche innere und äußere Denkbarrie- ren und Hindernisse überwunden. Mit dem Hochhaus- ensemble ist nicht nur eines der höchsten Häuser der Stadt Zürich entstanden, es sind zugleich die ersten Hochhäuser in der Stadt seit 20 Jahren. Die ersten Kon- zeptideen zu deren Bau waren schließlich Anlass für die Entwicklungsplanungen für das gesamte Quartier. Wahrlich, hier ist Pionierarbeit geleistet worden. Weit- sichtig. Nachhaltig. Flexibel.
Es ist der Architektengemeinschaft atelier ww und Max Dudler zu verdanken, dass eine gestalterische Vision von derart bestechender Klarheit und Eindrücklichkeit auf den Weg gebracht werden konnte. Die Kraft der Architektur vermochte zwei unterschiedliche Investoren und zwei Ar- chitektenteams über 15 Jahre Planungs- und Bauzeit unter einer Idee zu versammeln. Und auch heute wirkt das Ensemble wie ein suggestives Logo, ein urbanes Sil- houettenbild als Emblem für den Wandel in Zürich-Nord. Die AXA Leben AG unterstreicht mit diesem repräsen- tativen Objekt ihr Vertrauen in die Stabilität des Schweizer

Beginning in 1856, Oerlikon profited from its location by the newly opened railway connection between Zurich and southern Germany. Owing to this advanta- geous location, the region became an important in- dustrial and trade area. Today, the railway line has become a major public transport axis, while the in- dustrial halls have since been replaced by »think tanks«. Since the end of the nineteen-nineties, the largest inner-city restructuring project in Switzerland is being implemented in Zurich Leutschenbach. Fol- lowing the relocation of the trade fair and the build- ing of the airport, the new Glattalbahn rapid transit rail system is a further forward-looking step that will benefit Leutschenbach – and thus also the high-rise ensemble on Thurgauerstrasse. Quadro-Platz, the square that lies halfway between the airport and the financial centre around Paradeplatz, will gain greater awareness amongst the Zurich inhabitants.
The excellent conditions of the transport hub at the corner of Thurgauerstrasse and Hagenholzstrasse were identified at an early stage by Implenia Devel- opment AG, and optimally developed with the AXA Leben AG and BVK. Investors, project developers, ar- chitects, and the Zurich municipal authorities overcame a number of internal and external thought barriers and obstacles on the way to completing the construction. The high-rise ensemble is not only one of the tallest groups of buildings in the city of Zurich, but also the first high-rise buildings to be built in the city for twenty years. The initial construction concepts were ulti- mately the basis for the development plans for the whole district. It is truly an example of pioneering work. Forward-looking, sustainable, flexible.
It is thanks to the architectural partnership of atelier ww and Max Dudler that such an exceptionally clear and impressive design vision could be realized. The power of architecture brought together two different investors and two architectural teams over a planning and con- struction period spanning fifteen years. Still today, the ensemble looks like a suggestive logo – an urban sil- houette as an emblem for change in Zurich-Nord. With this representative object, AXA Leben AG demon- strates its faith in the stability of the Swiss market and in the attractiveness of Zurich as an economic centre. On behalf of AXA Leben AG, I would like to

d

Marktes und in die Attraktivität des Wirtschaftsplatzes Zürich. Im Namen der AXA Leben AG spreche ich meinen großen Dank an all jene aus, die zur Realisierung beigetragen haben. Ich wünsche unseren Mitarbeitenden und Mietern, dass sie sich in dieser qualitativ hervorragenden Umgebung wohlfühlen mögen.

e

express my enormous gratitude to all those who contributed to the realization of this project. I hope that all of our employees and tenants will enjoy these high-quality surroundings.

Silhouette des Hochhausensembles vom Bahnhof Oerlikon aus gesehen
Silhouette of the high-rise ensemble seen from Oerlikon train station

Blick aus der Leutschenbachstrasse
View from Leutschenbachstrasse

Eine Stadt in der Stadt
Über urbanes Bauen in der Peripherie

Einführung der Herausgeber
Alexander Bonte und J. Christoph Bürkle

A City within the City
On Urban Development in the Periphery

Introduction by the editors
Alexander Bonte and J. Christoph Bürkle

d

e

**Douglas DC-3-216 im Flug über der offenen Rennbahn
und dem Hallenstadion in Oerlikon, 1937**
Douglas DC-3-216 flying over the open racetrack
and the Hallenstadion events venue in Oerlikon, 1937

Eine Schwarzweißaufnahme aus dem Jahr 1937 zeigt den silbernen Rumpf einer zweimotorigen Douglas DC-3 über dem heutigen Grundstück des Hochhausensembles an der Thurgauerstrasse. Im Hintergrund ist neben der offenen Radrennbahn das im Bau befindliche Hallenstadion zu sehen; ein Bahndamm quert das Bild, es ist die Nordostbahn, die Zürich und das seit 1934 zu Zürich gehörende Oerlikon mit dem Bodensee verbindet. Ansonsten ist zu sehen, was dieser Teil von Zürich 1937 nicht war: eine der dynamischsten Regionen der Schweiz, in deren Mitte hier einmal das dritthöchste Haus der Stadt stehen wird.

In wenigen Jahrzehnten hat das durch ländliche Strukturen geprägte Territorium eine außergewöhnliche Entwicklung vollzogen. Im Sog des boomenden Flughafens Kloten ist über den Hinterlassenschaften der großen Maschinenfabriken, die sich hier in einem ersten Schub der Modernisierung an der Eisenbahnstrecke niedergelassen hatten, ein neuer Anziehungspol für die gesamte Schweiz entstanden, eine europäische »Edge City« oder »Airport City« [in Anlehnung an den Begriff, den Joel Garreau zur Beschreibung der neuen Zentren neben den großen amerikanischen Metropolen eingeführt hat], die sich anschickt, den Central Business District der Kernstadt Zürich in Bezug auf Büroflächen, Geschäftszentren und Anzahl der Hauptsitze nationaler und internationaler Unternehmen zu überflügeln.

Mitten in diesem Stadtagglomerat, bestehend aus auf sich selbst bezogenen Parzellen mit anscheinend willkürlich nebeneinander angehäuften Formen und Funktionen, hat die Arbeitsgemeinschaft atelier ww und Max Dudler ein Gebäudeensemble errichtet, welches sich in radikaler Weise mit dieser neuen Form der Stadt auseinandersetzt. Das Hochhausensemble an der Thurgauerstrasse ist ebenfalls als selbstbezogene Insel – als Stadt in der Stadt – geplant.

Seine Konzeption erscheint so einfach, dass man seine Disposition schon auf den ersten Blick vollständig zu begreifen glaubt. Vier Türme auf quadratischem Grundriss sind auf einem ebenfalls fast quadratischen Rasterfeld um einen rechtwinkligen Platz angeordnet. Alle Türme wachsen aus einer niedrigeren Sockelbebauung empor, die durch verschieden schmale Gassen durchbrochen wird, welche sich mit dem Wegenetz der Stadt verbinden. Im Aufriss zeichnet sich eine Dreiteilung ab: eine Ebene

A black-and-white photograph from the year 1937 shows the silver fuselage of a twin-engined Douglas DC-3 over the present-day site of the high-rise ensemble on Thurgauerstrasse. In the background, next to the open cycle race track, one can see the Hallenstadion events hall in the process of being built. A railroad embankment traverses the picture; it is the northeast track that connects Zurich – and Oerlikon, which has been part of Zurich since 1934 – to Lake Constance. Apart from this, one can see what this part of Zurich had not yet become in 1937: one of the most dynamic regions of Switzerland, at whose center the third highest building in the city would stand one day.

Within just a few decades, the territory characterized by rural structures has undergone a remarkable transformation and development. In the wake of the booming Kloten airport, a new magnet for the whole of Switzerland has been created on the site of the remains of the large engineering works that had been established here during the first phase of modernization along the railroad tracks. It is a European »edge city« or »airport city« [referring to the term that Joel Garreau introduced to describe the new urban centers next to the major American metropolises], which is aiming to surpass the Central Business District in the city center of Zurich in terms of office spaces, business centers, and the number of head offices of national and international companies.

In the midst of this urban agglomerate, consisting of a cluster of self-referential sites with seemingly arbitrarily juxtaposed forms and functions, the work group of atelier ww and Max Dudler has erected a building ensemble that reasserts this new city form in a radical way. The high-rise ensemble on Thurgauerstrasse is designed as a self-referential island – as a city within the city.

The concept behind it appears so simple that its disposition seems comprehensible at first glance. Four towers with a square layout are arranged around a rectangular space on an almost square grid. All the towers grow out of a lower base construction, which is broken up by varying narrow alleys, according to the dimensional specifications of the grid. These alleys are linked to the infrastructural network of the surrounding city.

d

der Fußgänger, die sich zum Platz hin dreiseitig als zweigeschossige Kolonnaden abzeichnet, darüber ein Bauvolumen, das übergreifend eine Traufkante hält – die Ebene der Stadt, – und wiederum darüber eine Hochhauskrone, die sich als Silhouette schon vom nahen Flughafen aus abzeichnet. Mit spielerischer Leichtigkeit entsteht eine städtebauliche Skulptur, an der nichts zufällig ist und nichts beliebig. Man kann nur vermuten, dass es gerade die indifferente Erscheinung der Peripherie war, die dieses Höchstmaß an Präzision, Einheit und Klarheit provoziert hat. Ja es scheint fast, als hätte das hier anzutreffende Konglomerat von Autohäusern, Sportplätzen, Bahntrassen und kleinteiligen Wohnüberbauungen diese überdeutliche Struktur erwartet. Doch die Bilder, die diese Stadtskulptur evoziert, changieren. Was im einen Moment als Balkendiagramm einer Tabellenkalkulation erscheint, erfährt das Auge im nächsten als Schimäre einer italienischen Architektur, als hätte sie ein de Chirico in einer ›pittura metafisica‹ festgehalten. Auch die geradezu monomane Wiederholung ein und desselben Fassadenmotivs aus steinernen Balken und Pfeilern entfaltet vor Ort eine irritierende Sinnlichkeit. Abstraktion oder Sinnlichkeit? Abstraktion und Sinnlichkeit!

Wie so oft trügt der Schein der Einfachheit: Dieser Monolith, der aus einer Idee, einem Detail und einem Material in unerschütterlicher Konsequenz zusammengefügt wurde, ist eine Ausnahme. Ein geradezu unwahrscheinliches Projekt – umso mehr, wenn man weiß, dass hier zwei Architekten und zwei Bauherren über fast 15 Jahre an der Realisierung dieser Vision gearbeitet haben. Während am Alexanderplatz in Berlin 15 Jahre nach dem Masterplan von Hans Kollhoff kein einziges Hochhaus steht, wirkt das Ensemble in Zürich-Nord wie ein 1:1-Mockup der Wettbewerbskonzeption. Wie ist so etwas möglich? Welche Bedingungen und Ideen haben die Realisierung des Hochhausensembles an der Thurgauerstrasse beeinflusst? Die Antworten, die wir hier zusammengetragen haben, sind alle mit diesem Ort verbunden: Die Peripherie ist der vielleicht einzige Ort, an dem eine derartig radikale Architektur überhaupt möglich ist.

Peripherie
»Die annähernd perfekte Peripherie« hat Mario Campi diesen Flickenteppich scheinbar wahllos aufeinander-

e

The elevation shows a trisection: a level for pedestrians, marked by two-story colonnades on three sides facing the square, then a building mass above it at the height of the eaves – the level of the city that forms the solid fabric of every city – and even higher above that a high-rise crown, visible as a silhouette even from the nearby airport. With almost playful ease, an urban sculpture is formed that is by no means coincidental or haphazard. One can only assume that it was precisely the indifferent appearance of the periphery that provoked this high degree of precision, uniformity, and clarity. It almost seems as if the conglomerate of car dealerships, sports grounds, railroads, and small-scale, mixed residential developments had been awaiting this predominant structure for a long time.

However, this monumental city sculpture evokes changing images. What appears one moment as a bar chart of a banal spreadsheet, is perceived by the eye the next as a chimera of some Italian architecture, as if de Chirico had captured it in a ›pittura metafisica‹. The virtually monomaniacal repetition of one and the same façade motif of stone beams and columns gives the site an almost irritating sensuality. Abstraction or sensuality? Abstraction and sensuality!

In many cases, the impression of simplicity is an illusion, but this monolith – composed of an idea, a detail, and a material, with unwavering consistency – is an exception. It is an unlikely project – all the more so considering that two architects and two clients worked on the realization of this vision for nearly fifteen years. While there is still not a single high-rise building on Alexanderplatz in Berlin, fifteen years after the pioneering master plan by Hans Kollhoff, the ensemble in Zurich-Nord appears as a 1:1 mock-up of the competition design. How is this possible? What conditions and ideas influenced the realization of the high-rise ensemble on Thurgauerstrasse? The answers to these questions, which we have brought together in this book, all point to this location in one way or another: the periphery is perhaps the only place where such a radical form of architecture is at all possible.

Periphery
»The almost perfect periphery« is what Mario Campi called this patchwork of seemingly randomly juxta-

**Fotoserie »Thurgauerstrasse«
von Olivia Heussler, Zürich**
»Thurgauerstrasse« photo series
by Olivia Heussler, Zurich

d

Mario Campi, Franz Bucher, Mirko Zardini:
›Annähernd perfekte Peripherie:
Glattalstadt/Greater Zurich Area‹. Zürich/Zurich 2000

treffender Stadtfragmente in Zürichs Norden genannt, eine »reife Peripherie«, welche die negativen Aufladungen des Begriffs [mit Assoziationen wie Ausschluss, Verwahrlosung, Armut, Marginalisierung] anscheinend hinter sich gelassen hat, um sich heute zu einem Labor der Zukunft für die Region zu entwickeln.

Diese Gegenwartsstadt, so seine Analyse, folgt keinem über einen langen Zeitraum verfolgten Gesamtplan, sondern ist einem komplexen, quasi natürlichen System der Selbstorganisation unterworfen. Doch während die Stadtforschung noch die Prozesse, die ihre Entwicklung beeinflussen, zu verstehen versucht, müssen sich Architekten dem Phänomen von Anfang an mit ganz konkreten Strategien annähern. Die möglichen Beziehungen, die Architektur in der Peripherie [oder Zwischenstadt oder Agglomeration] zum Ort, zur Zeit und auch zur Geschichte aufnehmen kann, unterscheiden sich grundlegend von den Bedingungen in der historischen Stadt. Das vorliegende Buch will zeigen, wie gleichsam radikal und folgerichtig die Architektengemeinschaft atelier ww und Max Dudler auf diese Bedingungen reagiert hat und wie anschlussfähig die mit dem Hochhausensemble geschaffenen Lösungen bezogen auf ähnliche Bedingungen sind.

Stadtlandschaft

Im Gegensatz zur westlichen Zürcher Peripherie, dem Ort der ersten Industrieansiedlungen entlang der Limmat, folgt Zürich-Nord einem anderen Modell der städtischen Entwicklung. Während in Zürich-West typische Assimilationsprozesse stattfinden, in deren Rahmen die alten Fabriken Zug um Zug in die urbane Struktur integriert werden, wächst der Norden als Mosaik städtischer Fragmente zunehmend größeren Maßstabs. Diese Stadtlandschaft wird primär durch die Adern der Infrastruktur organisiert und zusammengehalten. Das Wachstum der Agglomeration folgt nicht dem Leitbild der kompakten europäischen Stadt mit ihren kontinuierlichen öffentlichen Räumen. Die Eigenschaften dieser neuen Stadt – wie der ständige Maßstabswechsel, die Kontraste [der Dimension und des Charakters] zwischen den auf sich selbst bezogenen Inseln – lassen sich zwar beschreiben, doch sind sie nicht willkürlich herbeigeführt und darüber hinaus durch ein rasantes Wachstum dem ständigen Wandel unterworfen.

e

posed city fragments in the north of Zurich, a »mature periphery«, which has apparently left the negative connotations of the term behind [such as exclusion, desolation, poverty, marginalization], evolving into a present-day laboratory for the future of the region. This contemporary city, according to his analysis, does not adhere to any long-term, overall plan, but is subject to a complex, quasi-natural system of self-organization. However, while urban research is still seeking to understand the processes that influence its development, architects have to approach the phenomenon from the outset with very concrete strategies. The possible references that architecture in the periphery [or conurbation or agglomeration] can make to its location, its time, as well as history, differ significantly from the situation in historic cities. This book seeks to show how radically and consequentially the architectural alliance of atelier ww and Max Dudler reacted to this situation and how compatible the solutions presented by the high-rise ensemble are when applied to similar situations.

Urban Landscape

In contrast to the western Zurich periphery, the site of the first industrial settlements along the Limmat, Zurich-Nord is following a different urban development model. While Zurich-West is experiencing typical urban assimilation processes, whereby the old factories are being integrated step by step into the urban structure, the north is growing as a mosaic of urban fragments on an increasingly large scale. This urban landscape of seemingly arbitrarily juxtaposed forms and functions is primarily organized and held together by the infrastructural arteries. The growth of the agglomeration is evidently no longer following the model of the compact European city, with its continuity of public spaces. The characteristics of this new city – such as the constant change of scale, the contrasts [in dimension and character] between the self-referential urban islands – can be described, but they are not brought about intentionally, and furthermore they are subject to constant change on account of rapid growth.

The first and strongest impression that the towers on Thurgauerstrasse make – namely that they are per-

d

Der erste und stärkste Eindruck, den die Türme an der Thurgauerstrasse vermitteln – nämlich ihre Wahrnehmung als städtische Einheit, die wie eine Insel in der Stadtlandschaft liegt –, thematisiert also gewissermaßen die primären strukturellen Bedingungen dieser Form der Stadt. Die Idee der urbanen Insel wird hier als architektonische Strategie benutzt. In einer Stadt, deren Gesicht keine konturierte Vergangenheit und eine noch weniger vorhersehbare Zukunft hat, muss eine Entwicklung dieser Größenordnung eine eigene Ordnung etablieren. Die schiere Größe schlägt in eine eigene Qualität um: Aus Architektur wird Urbanismus.

Stadt in der Stadt

Es ist nicht ohne Ironie, dass die Architekten in dieser Region des manischen Wachstums eine Strategie gewählt haben, die derjenigen ähnelt, welche Oswald M. Ungers anlässlich der Berliner Sommerakademie der Cornell University im Jahr 1977 zur Bewältigung der Probleme der seinerzeit schrumpfenden Stadt Berlin propagiert hat. Die »City within a City« ist Ungers radikaler Vorschlag, Berlin auf einzelne urbane Archipele zurückzubauen. Durch das Herausarbeiten der Identität dieser – durch architektonische Klarheit und physiognomische Lesbarkeit – herausragenden Stadtfragmente sollte Berlin nach Ungers' Konzept zu einer Stadt der Identitäten entwickelt werden [im Gegensatz zur Einheitsidee von der Stadt]. Für Ungers kommt es dabei darauf an, Vielfalt und Eindeutigkeit gleichermaßen zu ermöglichen, denn dies stellt für ihn den eigentlichen Sinn pluralistischer Freiheit dar. Das Zusammentreffen der Gegensätze soll sich gegenseitig bereichern, anstatt sich aufzuheben. Hierfür ist zum einen erforderlich, dass jedes einzelne Stadtfragment physiognomisch wie typologisch vollendet entwickelt ist, zum anderen kommt den Rändern, Grenzen und Übergängen eine besondere Rolle zu. Das Ensemble von atelier ww und Max Dudler ist ebenfalls von Anfang an als Fragment entwickelt, als physiognomisch wie typologisch gedachte Stadt in der Stadt. Während in Ungers' Konzeptentwurf die Übergänge zwischen den Inseln durch eine Grünlandschaft markiert werden, welche der Stadtlandschaft komplementär entgegengesetzt wird, lösen die Architekten des Ensembles das Problem der Grenze geometrisch: Die reine Geometrie der Architektur steht gegen die dynamische Geometrie der Verkehrs-

e

ceived as an urban unity, which lies like an island within the urban landscape – therefore indicates to a certain extent the primary structural conditions of this form of city. The idea of the urban island is used as a genuine architectural strategy here. In a city whose face does not have a defined past, nor a predictable future, a development on this scale ultimately has to establish its own order. The sheer size requires a particular quality: architecture becomes urbanism.

City within the City

It is not without irony that the architects in this region of manic growth have chosen a strategy similar to the one propagated by Oswald Mathias Ungers on the occasion of the Berlin Summer Academy held by Cornell University in 1977 to overcome the problems of the shrinking city of Berlin of his time. The »city within a city« was Ungers's radical proposal for scaling Berlin back to individual urban archipelagos. By establishing the identity of these city fragments, which were prominent due to their architectural clarity and physiognomic readability, Berlin was to be developed into a city of identities, according to Ungers's concept [as opposed to the concept of the city as uniform]. For Ungers, it was about enabling both diversity and unambiguity, as in his opinion this was what pluralistic freedom was all about. The coming together of contrasts was to be mutually enriching, instead of one neutralizing the other. This requires, first of all, that each individual city fragment is fully developed physiognomically and typologically, while an important role is also played by edges, borders, and transitions. The ensemble by atelier ww and Max Dudler was also developed from the beginning as a fragment, as a physiognomical and typological city within the city. Whereas in the concept design by Ungers the transitions between the islands are marked by a green landscape, which is set against the urban landscape complementarily, the architects of the ensemble solve the problem of the border geometrically: the pure geometry of the architecture is set against the dynamic geometry of the infrastructural axes. This creates polygonal outer areas that have a particular spatial design, depending on their orientation and function.

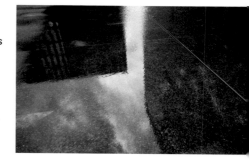

d

e

Gesamtansicht von der Bahntrasse
General view from the railroads

**Blick von der Kreuzung
Hagenholzstrasse/Thurgauerstrasse**
View from the junction of
Hagenholzstrasse/Thurgauerstrasse

achsen. Es entstehen polygonale Vorräume, sozusagen »Außenräume«, die je nach Orientierung und Funktion eine besondere Platzgestaltung erhalten.

Identität

Der Bezug zu Ungers' Stadt der Identitäten ist auch deswegen so virulent, weil das architektonische Problem der Agglomeration aufgrund des Fehlens signifikanter räumlicher, historischer oder inhaltlicher Determinanten ein Problem der Identität ist. Während der »Städtebau« der Agglomeration durch einen Mangel an Beziehungen, gemeinsamen Absichten und Regeln charakterisiert ist, hat Rem Koolhaas für ihre Architektur in seinem Text »Generic City« im Gegenteil das Problem der Konvergenz herausgearbeitet [»Is the contemporary city like the contemporary airport – all the same?«]. Analog zu Frank Lloyd Wright, der seiner Städtebau-Utopie »Broadacre City« das ›single-family detached home‹ als kleinste unteilbare Einheit zugrunde gelegt hatte, analysiert Koolhaas die Gegenwartsstadt als endlose Wiederholung des immer gleichen einfachen Moduls: »It is possible to reconstruct it from its smallest entity, a desktop computer, maybe even a diskette«. Die zweite auf den ersten Blick hervorstechende Eigenschaft der Hochhäuser an der Thurgauerstrasse, nämlich die monothematische Reihung eines Fassadenmotivs in einem Material und in einer Ordnung, erscheint aus dieser Perspektive ebenfalls als direkter Reflex auf die Bedingungen der Peripherie. Der Minimalismus dieser Architektur mag in einer Tradition von Max Bill bis Richard Serra gegründet sein, an diesem Ort weißt er über eine rein künstlerische Setzung hinaus. Die Repetition weniger, sorgfältig formulierter Details in den Fassaden entspricht der Wiederholung der einfachen Figur der Türme auf quadratischem Grundriss. Dabei ist die Architektur konsequent aus der ihr zugrunde liegenden Typologie entwickelt. Sie gaukelt nichts vor, sondern ist genau das, was sie ist. In diesem Punkt liegt ihre Identität. Und es ist gerade dieser Punkt, an dem die zurückhaltende, fast neutrale Form umschlägt: Sie wird zum Zeichen für diesen Ort. Das Silhouettenbild der Türme, die in ihrem Zentrum einen Platz aufnehmen, wird zu einem Bild für die Stadt. Wie ein Vexierbild wechselt die Figur zwischen Neutralität und Identität, zwischen Selbstbezüglichkeit und Kontextualität. Das Hochhausensemble

Identity

Another reason the reference to Ungers's city of identities is so virulent is because the architectural problem of the agglomeration is a problem of identity, due to the absence of significant spatial, historical, or contentual determinants. While the »urban development« of the agglomeration is characterized by a lack of references, common intentions and rules, Rem Koolhaas pointed out, on the contrary, the problem of convergence in his text »Generic City« [»Is the contemporary city like the contemporary airport – all the same?«]. Analogously to Frank Lloyd Wright, who had taken the single-family, detached home – the smallest indivisible unit – as the basis for his urban planning utopia »Broadacre City«, Koolhaas analyses the contemporary city as an endless repetition of the same simple formula: »It is possible to reconstruct it from its smallest entity, a desktop computer, maybe even a diskette.«

Apparent at first glance, the second feature of the high-rise buildings on Thurgauerstrasse is the monothematic sequence of a façade motif in one material and one arrangement, which from this perspective also appears as a direct reaction to the circumstances in the periphery. The minimalism of this architecture may be founded in a tradition from Max Bill to Richard Serra, but in this location it goes beyond a purely artistic stance. The repetition of few carefully formulated details on the façades corresponds to the repetition of the simple figure of the towers on a square layout. The architecture therefore evolves consistently from the typology it is based on. It does not make any pretenses, but is exactly what it is. Herein lies its identity.

It is precisely this that makes the modest, almost neutral form take on a new significance: it becomes emblematic of this location. The silhouette of the towers, with a square occupying the centre, forms an image of the city. Like a flip-flop picture, the figure alternates between neutrality and identity, between self-reference and contextuality. The high-rise ensemble is both an emblem and a building without characteristics in a city without a history. In this regard, it is scarcely surprising that no definitive name for the buildings has yet been able to establish itself.

d

ist beides zugleich – ein Wahrzeichen und ein Haus ohne Eigenschaften in einer Stadt ohne Geschichte.

Ensemble

Die Architekten haben immer wieder das Rockefeller Center in New York als zentrale Referenz für ihren Entwurf angegeben. Dessen ›lead-architect‹ Raymond Hood verstand das Center gleichfalls als »City within a City«. Die offensichtliche Lehre des Rockefeller Center besteht in der harmonischen Anordnung mehrerer Gebäude um einen zentralen Platz. Das eigentlich Neue an der Radio City ist, dass sie als Ensemble entwickelt wurde. Das sah auch Hood so: »As each individual structure will harmonize with the architecture of the group, so also will the decorations fit into an inclusive ornamental plan to tell, in the symbolic language of the arts, a connected understandable story«. Auf diese Weise implantieren Hood und seine Mitstreiter ein Lehrstück europäischen Stadtverständnisses in das ›grid‹ von New York. Doch wie das Rockefeller Center ein Import ist, so ist das Hochhausensemble ein Reimport amerikanisch-europäischer Hochhauskultur in einen amerikanisierten, europäischen »Strip«. Wie das Rockefeller Center wurde die Hochhausgruppe an der Thurgauerstrasse als Ensemble entworfen, dessen Platzräume den gleichen Rang haben wie die Objekte selbst. Noch mehr als beim Rockefeller Center ordnet sich die Architektur der städtebaulichen Figur unter. Die Figur erscheint als Bild, fast wie eine Skulptur.

Geschichte

Es erscheint offensichtlich, dass die Geschichte der Architektur auf diesem Binnenplatz im Zentrum dieser Häuser präsent ist. Doch es ist schwer nachzuvollziehen, auf welchem Wege diese Präsenz hergestellt wird. Eine derartig abstrakte Architektur lässt sich nicht so leicht auf irgendein Bild oder Vorbild zurückführen. Die strukturelle Ähnlichkeit eines Idealstadtentwurfes von Albrecht Dürer aus der Renaissance mit dem Grundriss des Ensembles gibt aber eine Ahnung davon, wie tief diese Figur im Bildreservoire der Architektur verankert ist. Geschichte wird hier nicht als Ressource verbraucht, sie erscheint vielmehr lebendig präsent – und dies gerade in dem Maße, wie die Architektur gerade ihren profanen Anlass ernst nimmt: als Typologie. Das Allgemeine ist ihr Besonderes.

e

Ensemble

The architects repeatedly cited Rockefeller Center in New York as the central reference for their design. Its lead architect Raymond Hood also understood the Center as a »city within a city«. The lesson taught by Rockefeller Center was the careful and harmonious arrangement of several buildings around a central square. What is actually novel about Radio City is that it was conceived as an ensemble. That is also how Hood saw it: »As each individual structure will harmonize with the architecture of the group, so also will the decorations fit into an inclusive ornamental plan to tell, in the symbolic language of the arts, a connected understandable story.« In this way, Hood and his colleagues implanted a piece of European urban understanding into the grid of New York. However, in the same way that Rockefeller Center is an import, the high-rise ensemble is a reimport of American-European high-rise culture into an Americanized, European »strip«. Like Rockefeller Center, the high-rise group on Thurgauerstrasse was designed as an ensemble, whose outdoor squares carry the same importance as the buildings themselves. Even more so than with Rockefeller Center, the architecture is subordinate to its presence within the urban context. This presence appears as a figure, almost as a sculpture.

History

It seems evident that the history of the architecture around this inner square at the center of the buildings has a greater presence than on many other sites. However, it is difficult to comprehend how this presence is generated. Such abstract architecture cannot easily be traced back to a particular image or model. The structural similarity of the ensemble's layout to an ideal city plan by Albrecht Dürer from the Renaissance, however, gives an indication of how deeply this figure is anchored in the imagery pool of architecture. History is not used here as a resource, but instead gives it a vibrant presence, showing that architecture is taking its secular purpose seriously, as a typology. The general is what makes it special.

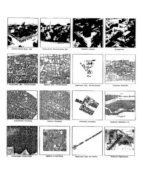

Oswald Mathias Ungers u. a./et. al. »Cities within the City: Proposals by the Sommer Akademie for Berlin«, 1977
Vergleich der Städtestruktur:
Comparison of urban structure:
a — urbane Inseln, Städte in einer Stadt, historische Beispiele
urban islands, cities within a city, historic examples
b — Friedrichstadt Süd – Karlsruhe
c — Görlitzer Bahnhof – Central Park New York
d — Unter den Eichen – Magnitogorsk

Oswald Mathias Ungers u. a./et. al. »Cities within the City: Proposals by the Sommer Akademie for Berlin«, 1977
Plan der Stadtinseln / Plan of urban islands

Albrecht Dürer
Quadratischer Idealstadtentwurf, 1527
Square design for an ideal city, 1527

Quadro-Platz: steinerner Platz, Poller, Wasserspiele
Quadro Square: stone square, bollards, water features

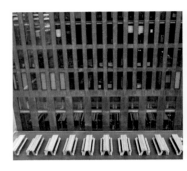

Quadro-Platz: Arkarden, Gassen, Eingänge
Quadro Square: arcades, alleys, entrances

Das urbane Hochhausensemble

Wolfgang Sonne

The Urban High-rise Ensemble

Wolfgang Sonne

d

Eine zusammenklingende Gruppe von Hochhäusern und keine unstimmige Ansammlung exzentrischer Einzelbauten, ein sich in die Stadt einfügendes Ensemble und kein strukturalistisches Cluster als Gegenmodell zur Stadt, ein städtischer Platz im Block und keine private Maximalausnutzung des Baugrunds: All diese Merkmale des Hochhausensembles an der Thurgauerstrasse in Zürich-Oerlikon von atelier ww und Max Dudler erscheinen als naheliegende Lösung für den Entwurf einer Gruppe von Hochhäusern in der Stadt – und sind doch so selten.

Denn Hochhäuser sind seltsame Gestalten. Wie Parasiten neigen sie dazu, das zu zerstören, was sie hervorbringt: das Städtische. Das mag befremdlich klingen, sind doch Hochhäuser keinesfalls der ländlichen Sphäre zugehörig, sondern die Frucht einer entwickelten städtischen Kultur. Und doch: zumeist drangsalieren sie das, was den Kern des Städtischen ausmacht – den öffentlichen Raum. Denn in seiner recht kurzen Geschichte seit der Erfindung des Aufzugs oszilliert das Hochhaus zwischen zwei Polen, die beide das Ende des öffentlichen Stadtraums bedeuten.

Der eine Pol liegt im radikal unternehmerischen Eigennutz, in der kapitalistischen Maximalverwertung der Immobilie zu privaten Zwecken – ohne Rücksicht auf die Umgebung, die Nachbargrundstücke und den öffentlichen Raum. So ist das Hochhaus im profitorientierten Chicago des ausgehenden 19. Jahrhunderts entstanden – und es war der radikale Eigennutz des Equitable Life Insurance Building in New York [1913–15], das mit seiner das Grundstück maximal ausnutzenden Baumasse die umliegenden Grundstücke in den Schatten stellte, der den öffentlichen Gesetzgeber zwang, tätig zu werden: Das New Yorker Zoning Law von 1916, das die Gebäudehöhen mit Rücksicht auf Nachbarn und Passanten regelte, war die Folge.

Der andere Pol liegt in der sozialistischen Bodenpolitik eines undefinierten Allgemeinbesitzes – ohne Verständnis für die komplexen Abstufungen des Öffentlichen und Privaten im städtischen Raum. Das Hochhaus im Grünen, ohne Bezug zur Straße im ›floating space‹ einer allgemein zugänglichen Grünfläche schwimmend, war hier das Leitbild einer sich meist auch sozialreformerisch gebärdenden Moderne. Suggestiv stellte Hendricus Theodorus Wijdeveld diese Vision 1919 mit seinem

e

A coherent group of high-rises rather than a dissonant collection of eccentric individual buildings, an ensemble of high-rises that blends into the city instead of a structuralist cluster as a countermodel to the city, an urban square within the block instead of maximum private usage of the site: all of these characteristics of the high-rise ensemble on Thurgauerstrasse in Zurich-Oerlikon by atelier ww and Max Dudler seem to be an obvious solution for the design of a group of high-rises within the city – and yet they are such a rarity.

High-rises are strange entities. Like parasites, they tend to destroy what sustains them: the urban environment. That might sound outlandish, but high-rises are by no means a natural phenomenon, instead they are the fruit of a developed urban culture. Even so, in most cases they gnaw away at what represents the core of urbanity – public space. This is because in their relatively short history – since the invention of the lift – high-rises oscillate between two poles, both of which represent the end of public urban space.

One pole is that of radically entrepreneurial self-interest, the capitalist maximum utilization of the building for private purposes – with no regard for the surroundings, the neighbouring sites, or the public space. This is how the high-rise emerged in the profit-oriented Chicago of the late nineteenth century, and it was the radical self-interest of the Equitable Life Insurance Building in New York [1913–15] – with a building mass that utilized its plot to the full and blocked daylight to the surrounding plots – that forced the municipal authorities to take action. This resulted in the New York Zoning Law of 1916, which regulated the heights of buildings in relation to neighbours and passers-by.

The other pole is that of the socialist land policy of undefined public ownership – with no understanding of the complex gradations of the public and the private within the urban sphere. The high-rise surrounded by greenery, with no relation to the street, in the »floating space« of a publicly accessible green area, was the model for a modern era that to a large extent was also characterized by social reforms. Hendricus Theodorus Wijdeveld presented this vision suggestively in 1919 with his ideal plan for Amsterdam, which consisted

Südliche Gasse von der Thurgauerstrasse
Southern alley from Thurgauerstrasse

d

Idealplan für Amsterdam vor: nur wildwüchsige Wiesen-
landschaft und Wohnungen in Hochhäusern, sonst nichts,
keine Stadt mehr. Über die bekannteren idealen Stadt-
entwürfe Le Corbusiers sollte sich das Hochhaus im
Grünen bis zu den ubiquitären Sozialsiedlungen der
Nachkriegszeit in West und Ost verbreiten und schließlich jedem den Tod der Urbanität durch diesen Hoch-
haustyp vor Augen stellen.

Antistädtisch sind sie beide: der egoistische Innenstadt-
brummer ebenso wie der sozial gedachte Turm im Grünen.
Beide lösen sie die delikate Balance eines städtischen
Hauses mit seiner Umgebung und dem öffentlichen
Raum auf: der eine, indem er rücksichtslos den Nachbarn und die Öffentlichkeit dominiert; der andere, indem er den öffentlichen Raum gleich ganz in einen undefinierten Grünraum auflöst und sich damit selbst der
städtischen Umgebung beraubt.

Doch waren dies nicht die einzigen Möglichkeiten in
der bislang 130-jährigen Geschichte des Hochhauses.
Schon sehr bald nach den ersten Exzessen des privat-
spekulativen Hochhausbaus machten sich Architekten
Gedanken, wie dieser neue Bautyp in die städtische
Bebauung integriert werden könnte, ohne sie durch
Dominanz zu zerstören. Und diese Bestrebungen, ur-
ban-zivilisierte Lösungen für das Hochhaus zu finden,
hielten auch an, als mit dem Turmhaus im Grünen
scheinbar die radikale Allzwecklösung gefunden war.
Hier werden nun einige solche Bestrebungen, einen
sehr großen Zuwanderer in die Gesellschaft der Stadt-
häuser nicht nur zu integrieren, sondern dabei auch
noch zum Auslöser für die Anlage schöner öffentlicher
Räume und urbaner Ensembles zu machen, geschil-
dert.[1]

In einem paradigmatischen Entwurf für die Chicago Lake
Front verband 1923 Eliel Saarinen Hochhäuser mit Plätzen und Straßen. Der erfahrene finnische Architekt und
Städtebauer hatte diese Studie im Nachgang zu seinem
Beitrag für den Chicago-Tribune-Tower-Wettbewerb von
1922, bei dem er mit einem bahnbrechenden Entwurf
den zweiten Preis errungen hatte, erarbeitet und gleichsam als Visitenkarte prominent in der Architekturzeit-
schrift The American Architect platziert. Saarinen näherte
sich der Planung von Chicago mit einem ästhetischen
Ziel. Er sah eine »abundant opportunity for monumental as well as picturesque development« und Chicagos

e

only of a proliferating meadow landscape and high-
rise blocks of apartments, nothing else, no town. According to the more well-known, ideal city plans by
Le Corbusier, the high-rise amidst greenery was to
spread as far as the ubiquitous social housing estates
of the post-war era in the west and in the east, and
ultimately present everyone with the death of urbanity.

Both of these poles are anti-urban: the egoistic inner-
city monolith, as well as the socialist block surrounded
by greenery. Both dissolve the delicate balance between a city residence on one side, and its surroundings and public space on the other: the former by
ruthlessly dominating the neighbours and the public
sphere, the latter by breaking up public space as a
whole into an undefined area of greenery, thereby
robbing itself of urban surroundings.

However, these were not the only alternatives in the
130-year history of the high-rise. Very soon after the
first excesses of private and speculative high-rise
construction, architects started to think about how this
new type of building could be integrated into the urban
surroundings, without destroying it with its domi-
nance. These endeavours to find urban and civilized
solutions for high-rises continued, even after a radical, comprehensive solution appeared to have been
found with the towering block surrounded by greenery. The following describes some of these attempts
not only to integrate such a massive immigrant into
the society of town houses, but also to make it a starting point for laying out beautiful public spaces and
urban ensembles.[1]

In a paradigmatic design for the Chicago Lake Front in
1923, Eliel Saarinen combined high-rises with squares
and streets. The experienced Finnish architect and
urban planner had developed this study subsequent
to his contribution to the Chicago Tribune Tower competition of 1922, for which he had won the second
prize with a groundbreaking design. It had given him
a prominent position in the architecture journal ›The
American Architect‹. Saarinen approached the planning of Chicago with an aesthetic goal in mind. He
saw »abundant opportunity for monumental as well
as picturesque development« and Chicago's chance
»of becoming in time one of the world's most beauti-

1
Vgl. Sonne, Wolfgang:
›Urbanität und Dichte im Städtebau
des 20. Jahrhunderts‹.
Berlin 2014

1
Cf. Wolfgang Sonne:
›Urbanität und Dichte im Städtebau
des 20. Jahrhunderts.‹
Berlin 2014.

Chance »of becoming in time one of the world's most beautiful cities.«[2] Für seine neuen Stadträume hatte er eine dezidiert urbane Vorstellung, die auf Burnhams Visionen von 1909 aufbaute: »A perspective sketch of Michigan Avenue, according to the Burnham plan, arises in my memory. I see elegant ladies and gentlemen promenading the Avenue in light, colorful costumes«.[3] Diese an Pariser Boulevards erinnernde Stimmung sollte seinen Stadtentwurf leiten.

Das Herzstück der Anlage war eine riesiger Platz, »a monumental open place – Grant Plaza – surrounded by flower beds and outside of them lower public buildings.«[4] [Abb. 1] Saarinen hatte sich für diese partielle Gestaltung von Grant Park als von Gebäuden gefassten Platz entschieden, da er kein »lonely monumental building in Grant Park« für öffentliche Zwecke wollte:

Zu den vergleichsweise niedrigen Rahmenbauten von Grant Plaza gesellte sich nun auch ein Hochhaus, das in die Wirkung der Platzrandbebauung mit einbezogen war: »In the background of Grant Plaza's North side and in line with Grant Boulevard, the previously mentioned hotel will rise, higher than the buildings on either side of it. Thus we attain a good rhythm and crescendo in the height relations.«[5] Das Hochhaus entspringt hier also nicht praktischen Anforderungen, die einen möglicherweise desaströsen Effekt auf den öffentlichen Stadtraum haben, sondern es ist vielmehr umgekehrt als ideales Gestaltungselement an einen öffentlichen Stadtraum gesetzt und erfüllt zufällig auch praktische Zwecke. Dabei ist seine städtebauliche Aufgabe dreifach: Es bildet den Kopf der riesigen Grant Plaza, auf deren ausgreifende Weite es mit einer entsprechenden Höhe antwortet; es bildet die Dominante der auf seiner nördlichen Seite gelegenen Central Plaza, in deren Randbebauung durch städtische Blöcke es geschickt einbezogen ist; [Abb. 2] und es bildet einen point de vue für Grant Boulevard, wo es durch seine von Ferne sichtbare Größe den Wahrnehmungsweisen des Autofahrers entspricht. So sehr die Grundform des Platzes von englischen Squares und französischen Places Royales herrührte, so sehr war hier doch durch die Dimensionen des neuen Bautyps ein ganz eigener großstädtischer Stadtraum entstanden, den in dieser Form zuvor weder Europa noch Amerika gekannt hatten.

ful cities«.[2] He had a distinctively urban vision for his new city spaces, based on Burnham's visions of 1909: »A perspective sketch of Michigan Avenue, according to the Burnham plan, arises in my memory. I see elegant ladies and gentlemen promenading the Avenue in light, colorful costumes.«[3] This atmosphere, evocative of Parisian boulevards, was to guide his plans for the city.

The centrepiece of the development was a gigantic square: »a monumental open place – Grant Plaza – surrounded by flower beds and outside of them lower public buildings«[4] [Ill. 1]. For his Grant Park design, Saarinen decided on a square surrounded by buildings, because he did not want a »lonely monumental building in Grant Park« for public purposes. The comparatively low surrounding buildings at Grant Plaza were joined by a high-rise, which formed part of the overall peripheral building development: »In the background of Grant Plaza's North side and in line with Grant Boulevard, the previously mentioned hotel will rise, higher than the buildings on either side of it. Thus we attain a good rhythm and crescendo in the height relations.«[5] Therefore, the high-rise was not determined by practical requirements, which can have a disastrous effect on public urban space, but on the contrary represented an ideal design element placed within a public urban setting that also happened to serve practical functions. His urban development project served a threefold purpose: it forms the head of the giant Grant Plaza, responding to its extensive width with a corresponding height; it represents the dominant feature of the Central Plaza on its northern side, integrated cleverly into its peripheral development of urban blocks [Ill. 2]; and it forms a ›point de vue‹ for Grant Boulevard, where its size – visible from afar – corresponds to the perceptions of motorists. Although the basic form of the square was derived from English squares and French »places royales«, the dimensions of the new type of building created a wholly new form of urban space, previously unknown in Europe or America.

Rockefeller Center in New York undoubtedly represents the most comprehensively conceived high-rise ensemble of the early twentieth century. It originally stemmed from plans for a new opera house and was a prime ex-

Abb. 2 / Ill. 2
**Eliel Saarinen,
Lake Front in Chicago,
Grant Hotel und/and Grant Plaza, 1923**

2
Saarinen, Eliel:
»Project for Lake Front Development of the City of Chicago«.
In: ›The American Architect. The Architectural Review‹. Bd. 124, H. 2434, 1923, S. 486–514, hier S. 487.
Vgl. Treib, Marc: »Eliel Saarinen as Urbanist: The Tower and the Square«.
In: ›Arkkitehti‹. H. 3,1985, S. 16–31;
Zukowsky, John [Hg.]: ›Chicago Architecture 1872–1922. Birth of a Metropolis‹.
München/London/New York 1987, S. 313–317

3
Saarinen, S. 488

4
Ebd., S. 502

5
Ebd., S. 502

2
Eliel Saarinen:
»Project for Lake Front Development of the City of Chicago.«
In: ›The American Architect. The Architectural Review‹. Vol. 124, No. 2434, 1923, p. 486–514, here p. 487.
Cf. Marc Treib: »Eliel Saarinen as Urbanist: The Tower and the Square.«
In: ›Arkkitehti.‹ No. 3, 1985, pp. 16–31;
John Zukowsky [Ed.]: ›Chicago Architecture 1872–1922. Birth of a Metropolis.‹ Munich/London/New York 1987, pp. 313–317.

3
Saarinen, p. 488.

4
Ibid., p. 502.

5
Ibid., p. 502.

d

e

**Abb. 3 / Ill. 3
Associated Architects
Rockefeller Center
in New York, 1931**

6
Dean, Henry H.:
»A New Idea in City Rebuilding«.
In: ›The American Architect‹.
Bd. 139, H. 2594, 1931,
S. 32–35 und 114, hier S. 33

7
Ebd., S. 34

8
Ebd., S. 33

6
Henry H. Dean:
»A New Idea in City Rebuilding.«
In: ›The American Architect.‹
Vol. 139, No. 2594, 1931,
pp. 32–35 and 114, here p. 33.

7
Ibid., p. 34.

8
Ibid., p. 33.

Das wohl umfassendste städtebaulich gedachte Hochhausensemble des frühen 20. Jahrhunderts bildet das Rockefeller Center in New York. Ursprünglich aus Planungen für ein neues Opernhaus hervorgegangen, ist es ein Musterbeispiel dafür, wie trotz strengster finanzieller Rahmenbedingungen mit dem Typus des Hochhauses qualitätvoller öffentlicher Stadtraum geschaffen werden konnte – ja, wie dieser selbst zu einer ökonomisch motivierten Strategie werden konnte. Denn was damals im gleichförmigen Raster von Manhattan fehlte, war ein für Fußgänger attraktiver städtischer Platz. Um sein neues Development auch in Zeiten der Wirtschaftskrise für potenzielle Kunden attraktiv zu machen, ließ John D. Rockefeller jr. auf privatem Grund gerade das anlegen, was die Umgebung nicht bot: öffentliche Räume. So entstanden inmitten des sich über drei Blöcke Manhattans erstreckenden Geländes eine Esplanade, die die Fußgänger von der 5th Avenue ins Herz der Anlage zog, und eine ›sunken plaza‹, die nicht allein einen vom Lärm der Stadt abgeschirmten locus conclusus schuf, sondern auch die Schaufensterfläch am Platz verdoppelte. Bemerkenswert ist vor allem, wie diese öffentlichen Räume durch die verschiedenen Projektphasen wanderten und letztlich zum Kerngedanken des ganzen Development wurden. Nach langen Vorplanungen präsentierte Rockefeller 1931 das Projekt einer Radio City mit verschiedenen Rundfunkgesellschaften als Ankermietern. Als Architekten zeichneten die drei Büros Reinhard & Hofmeister, Corbett, Harrison & MacMurray sowie Raymond Hood, Godley & Fouilhoux verantwortlich, die als Associated Architects zusammengefasst worden waren. [Abb. 3] Rockefeller war es gelungen, die ambitioniertesten und besten Architekten der Stadt in produktiver Konkurrenz an einem Projekt zusammenzubringen – entsprechend ehrgeizig, außergewöhnlich und durchdacht war das Ergebnis. Vielfältige Aktivitäten waren auf dem zentralen städtischen Grundstück vorgesehen und in eine einheitliche Baugruppe mit wohlgestalteten öffentlichen Räumen gepackt worden. Die zeitgenössische Kritik beschrieb das Projekt enthusiastisch als »one unified and interrelated group of buildings for the largest business, cultural, music and entertainment center in the world«,[6] das sich durch »multifarious activities« auszeichne[7]. Damit biete das Rockefeller Center »a more civic-minded attitude in the rebuilding of a city«.[8]

ample of how, despite strict financial constraints, high-quality urban spaces could be created by the high-rise building type. Indeed, this would even become an economically motivated strategy, because what was missing at the time in the uniform grid of Manhattan was urban space that was attractive for pedestrians. In order to make his new development attractive for potential clients, even in times of economic crisis, John D. Rockefeller, Jr. laid out on private ground what the surroundings did not yet have: public spaces. An esplanade was created in the middle of the site spanning three blocks in Manhattan, drawing pedestrians from 5th Avenue into the »heart« of the development, as well as a ›sunken plaza‹, which not only formed a ›locus conclusus‹ sheltered from the noise of the city, but also doubled the shop window surface on the square. It is particularly interesting to see how these public spaces threaded their way through the various project phases and ultimately became the core aspect of the whole development. After lengthy preliminary planning, in 1931 Rockefeller presented the project of a radio city, with various broadcasting companies as key tenants. Three architecture firms were appointed – Reinhard & Hofmeister, Corbett, Harrison & MacMurray, and Raymond Hood, Godley & Fouilhoux – who cooperated as associated architects [Ill. 3]. Rockefeller and his project had succeeded in bringing together the city's best and most ambitious architects in productive competition with each other and the result was suitably ambitious, unusual, and well planned. The central urban site was designed for a wide range of activities, incorporated into a coherent group of buildings with well-designed public spaces. The project was heralded enthusiastically at the time as »one unified and interrelated group of buildings for the largest business, cultural, music, and entertainment center in the world«,[6] characterized by »multifarious activities«.[7] Thus, Rockefeller Center represented »a more civic-minded attitude in the rebuilding of a city«.[8]

Despite many changes of plan, the complex was realized at breathtaking speed. The central buildings were built as early as 1933 and the development was completed in 1939. Its main attraction undoubtedly lay in the new public spaces, the esplanade, and especially

Realisiert wurde der Komplex trotz weiterer mehrfacher Planwechsel in atemberaubendem Tempo: Schon 1933 waren die zentralen Bauten fertiggestellt, 1939 war die Anlage vollendet. Die Hauptattraktion lag zweifelsfrei in den neuen öffentlichen Räumen, der Esplanade und vor allem der zentralen ›sunken plaza‹, mit denen Rockefeller nicht nur Besucher und Kunden anlocken, sondern auch Mieter aus weniger attraktiven Büros abwerben wollte. [Abb. 4] Mit unverblümter Deutlichkeit erläuterte Raymond Hood, der führende Entwerfer im Team der Architekten, die ökonomischen Bedingungen für die Konzeption des Platzes. Zunächst galt es, soviel Geschäftsfläche im Erdgeschossbereich wie möglich zu schaffen: »Since street level space in this district earns many times as much as office space in the upper stories, one of the guiding principles in the plan was to obtain the maximum ground floor area and street perimeter.«[9] Dafür wurde auch das Souterrain als Verkaufsebene konzipiert, erschlossen durch einen Platz, der ihm als ›sunken plaza‹ die Vorteile einer tieferliegenden Erdgeschossebene verschaffte. Hier ist der qualitätvoll gestaltete öffentliche Raum nicht die Folge finanzieller Prosperität mit einem gesellschaftlichen Ziel, sondern – umgekehrt – das Mittel, um den privaten Profit zu erhöhen. Gleichwohl, im Prinzip der möglichst hohen Dichte an Verkaufs- und Büroflächen in Verbindung mit öffentlichen Räumen sah Hood nicht allein ein ökonomisch motiviertes Ziel, sondern eine generelle Qualität des städtischen Lebens: »It has been founded upon the principle that concentration in a metropolitan area for business reasons is a desirable condition. […] the commercial success of urban life is dependent upon concentration, which provides immediate access to those with whom we have to deal. […] Decentralization means loss of time and inconvenience.«[10] Während die Dezentralisierungsbemühungen, wie sie etwa zeitgleich die Regional Planning Association und Lewis Mumford unter dem Eindruck von Howards Garden City propagierten, Zeit- und damit Geldverlust durch lange Pendelfahrten hervorriefen, sei urbane Dichte und Konzentration ein Gebot der Ökonomie und eine Eigenschaft des urbanen Lebens.

So geschickt, wie die öffentlichen Räume angeordnet waren, so raffiniert artikulierte auch die sie bildende Bebauung den neuen städtischen Raum: Zur 5th Avenue

the central sunken plaza, with which Rockefeller wanted not only to attract visitors and customers, but also to entice tenants away from less attractive offices [Ill. 4]. Raymond Hood, the leading designer in the architectural team, gave a clear and frank explanation of the economic idea behind the concept of the square. First of all, it was designed to create as much commercial space as possible at ground floor level: »Since street-level space in this district earns many times as much as office space in the upper stories, one of the guiding principles in the plan was to obtain the maximum ground floor area and street perimeter.«[9] Therefore, the basement level was also designed as a commercial floor, accessed via the sunken plaza that gave it the advantage of being a lower-lying, ground-floor level. The well-designed public space was not the result of financial prosperity with a social objective, but a means of increasing private profit. Even so, Hood saw the principle of the highest possible density of commercial and office spaces combined with public spaces not only as an economically motivated goal, but also as advantageous for the quality of urban life: »It has been founded upon the principle that concentration in a metropolitan area for business reasons is a desirable condition.… the commercial success of urban life is dependent upon concentration, which provides immediate access to those with whom we have to deal.… Decentralization means loss of time and inconvenience.«[10] While the decentralization efforts – as propagated around the same time by the Regional Planning Association and Lewis Mumford, and inspired by Howard's Garden City – cost time and money due to long commuter distances, urban density and concentration were an economic imperative and integral to urban life.

Not only were the public spaces cleverly arranged, but the surrounding developments that shaped them also defined the new urban space. Facing 5th Avenue, mediating urban blocks of a conventional height framed the new pedestrian esplanade on a human scale. In the depths of the space, the central high-rise of the RCA building rose in vertical layers, in breathtaking contrast enhanced even further by the lowered sunken plaza in front of it. The good architecture also contributed to the effect of the squares and streets.

Abb. 4
Associated Architects,
›sunken plaza‹ des Rockefeller Center in New York, 1931

Ill. 4
Associated Architects,
›sunken plaza‹ of the Rockefeller Center in New York, 1931

9
Hood, Raymond:
»The Design of Rockefeller City«.
In: ›The Architectural Forum‹.
Bd. 56, H. 1, 1932, S. 37–60, hier S. 39

10
Ebd., S. 48

9
Raymond Hood:
»The Design of Rockefeller City«.
In: ›The Architectural Forum‹.
Vol. 56, No. 1, 1932, pp. 37–60, here p. 39.

10
Ibid., p. 48.

d

Abb. 5
Max Berg,
Hochhaus am Ring in Breslau, 1920

Ill. 5
Max Berg,
High-rise on the ring road, Wroclaw, 1920

11
Hood, Raymond:
»Rockefeller Center«.
In: ›Society of Beaux-Arts Architects Yearbook‹.
1933, S. 69–74.

12
Roussel, Christine:
›The Art of Rockefeller Center‹.
New York 2006.

13
Ilkosz, Jerzy/Störtkuhl, Beate [Hg.]:
›Hochhäuser für Breslau 1919–1932‹.
Delmenhorst 1998.

14
Berg, Max:
»Der Bau von Geschäftshochhäusern in
Breslau zur Linderung der Wohnungsnot«.
In: ›Stadtbaukunst alter und neuer Zeit‹.
Bd. 1, H. 7/8, 1920, S. 99–104, 116–118.

11
Raymond Hood:
»Rockefeller Center.«
In: ›Society of Beaux-Arts Architects
Yearbook‹. 1933, pp. 69–74.

12
Christine Roussel:
›The Art of Rockefeller Center.‹
New York 2006.

13
Jerzy Ilkosz and Beate Störtkuhl [Eds.]:
›Hochhäuser für Breslau 1919–1932.‹
Delmenhorst 1998.

14
Max Berg:
»Der Bau von Geschäftshochhäusern in
Breslau zur Linderung der Wohnungsnot.«
In: ›Stadtbaukunst alter und neuer Zeit.‹
Vol. 1, No. 7/8, 1920, pp. 99–104, 116–118.

vermittelten städtische Blöcke in gewöhnlicher Stadt-
höhe und rahmten die neue Fußgängeresplanade im
menschlichen Maßstab. In die Tiefe des Raumes staf-
felte sich das zentrale Hochhaus des RCA Building von
Hood auf – in seinem atemberaubenden Kontrast noch
gesteigert durch die vorgelagerte vertiefte ›sunken plaza‹.
Zur Wirkung der Plätze und Straßen trug ebenfalls die
gute Architektur bei. Die wertvolle Steinverkleidung
der Bauten begründete Hood lapidar mit der Haltbarkeit
und dauerhaften Schönheit des Materials, das somit
langfristig am kostengünstigsten sei.[11] Hinzu kam die
Ausstattung des ganzen Komplexes mit Kunstwerken
von der Bauornamentik über die Freiplastik bis hin zur
Wandmalerei – alles jedoch eingebunden in eine domi-
nierende architektonische Haltung, die das Detail zwar
schätzte, es aber als Teil des großen Ganzen einglieder-
te, womit jeder Eindruck von überbordender Reichhal-
tigkeit vermieden war.[12] Tatsächlich war mit dem Rockefeller Center der Beweis angetreten worden, dass das
Hochhaus nicht notwendig als Vernichter des Öffentlichen und Gemeinschaftlichen auftreten muss. Im Gegenteil: Hier hatte das Hochhaus die Anlage des Platzes finanziell ermöglicht, ihm dann aber auch durch
seine Gestalt in ganz eigener Weise zu einer neuen
Qualität verholfen. In diesem doppelten Sinne sind die
öffentlichen Räume des Rockefeller Center tatsächlich
eine Folge des Hochhausensembles.
In Europa verwendete der Breslauer Stadtbaurat Max
Berg das Hochhaus zum ersten Mal systematisch im
Rahmen einer realen Gesamtstadtplanung 1919–21
bei seinen Entwürfen für Breslau.[13] Dabei vertrat er die
Theorie, durch den Bau von Bürohochhäusern den nach
dem Krieg dringend benötigten Wohnraum kostengün-
stiger als durch neue Wohnanlagen zu gewinnen: Büro-
hochhäuser könnten im Zentrum der bestehenden Stadt
angelegt werden und würden so das Freiziehen von
durch Firmen belegte Wohnungen ermöglichen, ohne
dass Kosten für die Erschließung neuer Wohngebiete
anfallen würden.[14] Einen weiteren Vorteil sah er in der
ökonomisch notwendigen Verdichtung der Stadt: »Für
die städtische Arbeit, die sich nur in der Geschäftsstadt
abspielt – zu der ich also auch die kleinere gewerbliche
Arbeit rechne – ist starke Konzentrierung das Haupter-
fordernis. Der Gesichtspunkt: Zeit ist Geld, muss für
die Anlage dieses Teiles der Großstadt, für die Geschäfts-

e

The valuable stone revetting of the buildings was jus-
tified succinctly by Hood, who cited the durability and
lasting beauty of the material, which made it the most
cost-effective option in the long term.[11] Furthermore,
the whole complex was adorned with works of art,
from architectural ornamentation to free-standing
sculptures and wall paintings – all of which, however,
were subordinate to an overriding architectural approach that valued details, but saw them as part of a
larger whole, thereby avoiding giving any impression
of excessive abundance.[12] Rockefeller Center had indeed provided proof that a high-rise did not have to
be a destroyer of the public and the communal. On
the contrary: the high-rise had financially enabled the
creation of the square, and gave it a new quality
through its particular presence and form. In both
ways, the public spaces of Rockefeller Center are
actually a result of the high-rise ensemble.
In Europe, Max Berg, the Head of Municipal Planning
in Wroclaw, systematically used the high-rise for the
first time in his designs for Wroclaw, as part of a general urban development plan in 1919–21.[13] He advo-
cated the theory that the residential space urgently
needed after the war could be gained more cost-effec-
tively by building office high-rises, than by creating
new residential estates. Office blocks could be built in
the centre of the existing city and enable companies
to vacate buildings that could then be used for residential purposes, avoiding the cost of building new
residential areas.[14] Another advantage, in his opinion,
was the densification of the city out of economic ne-
cessity: »Dense concentration is the main prerequisite
for work in the city that is focussed on the commercial areas, which also includes smaller-scale commercial activities. The aspect of time is money has to play
a key role in the layout of this commercial part of the
city.… Therefore it cannot be denied that we are also
striving for a greater concentration within the commercial city, and given that this is not possible horizon-
tally within the built-up area, as the greater volume of
traffic requires wider streets, it can only happen verti-
cally.«[15] Hence, densification as a prerequisite for
urban commercial life required the building of high-
rises. Berg's actual achievement lay in the well-planned
integration of high-rise buildings into the urban fab-

d

stadt maßgebend sein. […] so ist doch nicht zu erkennen, dass auch wir nach einer größeren Konzentrierung der Geschäftsstadt hinstreben, und da dies in der bebauten Fläche nicht geschehen kann – da im Gegenteil der stärkere Verkehr größere Straßenbreiten erfordert, so kann dies nur nach der Höhe erfolgen.«[15] Verdichtung als Notwendigkeit städtischen Geschäftslebens erfordere somit die Anlage von Hochhäusern.

Bergs eigentliche Leistung lag in der städtebaulich reflektierten Einordnung der Hochhausbauten in das Stadtgefüge. Paradigmatisch stehen dafür sein mit Richard Konwiarz entworfenes Hochhaus am Lessingplatz, das am Ufer der Oder gelegen war, sowie sein mit Ludwig Moshamer entworfenes Hochhaus am Ring, das als neue Stadtkrone neben dem alten Rathaus den Breslauer Hauptplatz dominierte. [Abb. 5] Insbesondere dieser letzte Entwurf, wie auch bei den anderen Hochhäusern in mehreren Varianten vorgelegt, verdeutlicht die sowohl revolutionäre als auch evolutionäre Haltung Bergs zur Stadt: Zum einen steht das Hochhaus mit seinem Maßstabsbruch in radikalem Kontrast zu den umliegenden Bauten, zum anderen schließt es mit seinen Staffelungen direkt an das mittelalterliche Rathaus an, übernimmt in expressionistischer Überhöhung gar dessen Giebelelemente und vermittelt durch Arkaden im Erdgeschoss in traditioneller Weise zum öffentlichen Stadtraum des Rings. So neu und lautstark es daherkommt, so urban und geschichtsbezogen ist es doch zugleich. Allein, Bergs Gesamtplanung mit ihren Hochhäusern wurde von den politischen Gremien abgelehnt, sodass seine stadtraumprägenden Hochhausvisionen Papier blieben. Geblieben aber ist ebenfalls seine Forderung, das Hochhaus neben einer guten funktionalen und konstruktiven Durchbildung vor allem als künstlerisch-architektonische und städtebauliche Aufgabe zu sehen, »wobei die gestaltende Hand des künstlerisch empfindenden Architekten als Krönung der Aufgabe durch die Verleihung der Wesensart entsprechenden Form und durch die empfindsame Einordnung in das Platz- und Straßenbild erst den künstlerischen Kulturwert schafft.«[16] Dasselbe Motiv des Stadttores mit Doppeltürmen, das schon 1915 der junge Architekt Sven Wallander für Stockholm vorgeschlagen hatte, bildete später die Piazza Dante in Genua aus. Hier war im Zuge der vor allem verkehrstechnischen Neuordnung des Innen-

e

ric. Examples of this are his high-rise on Lessingplatz, designed with Richard Konwiarz, which was located on the Oder riverbank; and his high-rise on the ring road, designed with Ludwig Moshamer, which dominated the main square in Wroclaw as the new crown of the city, alongside the old town hall [Ill. 5]. The latter design, in particular, shows Berg's both revolutionary and evolutionary attitude towards the city, as do the other high-rises in various ways: on the one hand, the new scale of the high-rise stands in radical contrast to the surrounding buildings, on the other hand its tiers mediate directly with the medieval town hall and it even adopts its gable elements in the form of an expressionistic superelevation, with traditional arcades on the ground floor providing a transition to the public urban space of the ring road. While it is new and conspicuous, it is also part of the cityscape and relates to the historical setting.

However, Berg's grand plan was rejected by the political authorities, so his high-rise visions for defining the urban space remained on paper only. What has also remained as a legacy, however, is his bid to see the high-rise primarily as an artistic, architectural, and urban development undertaking, and not just as serving functional and structural purposes, whereby »the design touch of the artistically-minded architect is what creates artistic and cultural value, as the crowning aspect of the high-rise, by giving it the appropriate form and integrating it sensitively into the public space and streetscape«.[16]

The same motif of the city gate with double towers, which the young architect Svan Wallander had proposed for Stockholm back in 1915, was to shape Piazza Dante in Genoa later. As part of the restructuring, especially infrastructural, of the inner city area in front of the medieval Porta Soprana – in itself an unusually high double tower structure – a new square was laid out, where several roads met and flowed into the road tunnel that linked the eastern development areas around Piazza della Vittoria with the city centre.[17] The arch motif of the tunnel entrance was used in conjunction with the framing double towers to form a new city gate on a larger scale [Ill. 6]. In 1932, the plan for this square was presented as part of a regulatory plan for the city centre. The new square was dominated

Abb. 6
Marcello Piacentini, Giuseppe Rosso,
Hochhäuser an der Piazza Dante in Genua, 1935–40

Ill. 6
Marcello Piacentini, Giuseppe Rosso,
high-rises on Piazza Dante in Genoa, 1935–40

15
Berg, Max:
»Die städtebaulichen Beziehungen der Großstadt zu ihren Vororten«.
Vortragsmanuskript, Nachlass Max Berg, Deutsches Museum München, zit. nach: Ilkosz, Jerzy: »Hochhäuser für Breslau von Max Berg«.
In: Lampugnani, Vittorio Magnago/ Romana Schneider [Hg.]: ›Moderne Architektur in Deutschland 1900 bis 1950. Reform und Tradition‹. Stuttgart 1992, S. 200–219, hier S. 218

16
Berg, Max:
»Die deutsche Hochhausbauweise«.
In: ›Deutsche Bauhütte‹. 1922, S. 54–58, S. 58

15
Max Berg:
»Die städtebaulichen Beziehungen der Großstadt zu ihren Vororten.«
Presentation manuscript, Nachlass Max Berg, Deutsches Museum Munich, quoted in: Jerzy Ilkosz: »Hochhäuser für Breslau von Max Berg.«
In: Vittorio Magnago Lampugnani and Romana Schneider [Eds.]: ›Moderne Architektur in Deutschland 1900 bis 1950. Reform und Tradition.‹ Stuttgart 1992, pp. 200–219, here p. 218.

16
Max Berg:
»Die deutsche Hochhausbauweise.«
In: ›Deutsche Bauhütte.‹
1922, pp. 54–58, here p. 58.

d

e

17
Cevini, Paolo:
›Genova anni ´30. Da Labò a Danieri‹.
Genua 1989;
Cevini, Paolo:
›Piacentini a Genova. Il grattacielo dell´Orologio‹.
Genua 2001

18
O. A.: »Il nuovo piano regolatore del centro«.
In: ›Genova. Rivista Municipale‹. Februar 1932,
S. 143–154, S. 148.
Dt.: » ... ein Platz, der ausdrücklich durch
mehrspurigen Verteilungsverkehr und
durch intensiven Handel geprägt war.«

19
Ebd. Dt.: »Der Platz erweist sich am Ende
als die angemessene Lösung verschiedener
technischer Probleme – geplant als ein die
Fortbewegung erleichternder Knotenpunkt,
durch den definierte obligatorische Achsen
geleitet werden, der zugleich die komplexen
architektonischen Anforderungen an die
Symmetrie erfüllen kann.«

20
›Les sept tours de Moscou. Les tours babylo-
niennes du communisme. De zeven torens van
Moskou. De babylonische torens van het communisme. 1935–1950‹. Brüssel 2005.

17
Paolo Cevini:
›Genova anni ´30. Da Labò a Danieri.‹
Genoa 1989;
Paolo Cevini:
›Piacentini a Genova. Il grattacielo dell´Orologio.‹
Genoa 2001.

18
O. A.: »Il nuovo piano regolatore del centro.«
In: ›Genova. Rivista Municipale.‹
February 1932, pp. 143–154, here p. 148.
English translation: » ... a square that was
characterized in particular by multilane traffic
and dense commerce.«

19
Ibid. English translation: »The square ultimately proved to be the appropriate solution
to various technical problems – planned as a
hub to facilitate movement, through which
defined, obligatory axes were directed, and
which at the same time can fulfill the complex
architectural requirements in terms of sym-
metry.«

20
›Les sept tours de Moscou. Les tours baby-
loniennes du communisme. De zeven torens
van Moskou. De babylonische torens van het
communisme. 1935–1950.‹ Brussels 2005.

stadtbereichs vor der mittelalterlichen Porta Soprana – ihrerseits eine ungewöhnlich hohe Doppelturmanlage – ein neuer Platz angelegt worden, an dem sich mehrere Straßen bündelten und in den Straßentunnel mündeten, der die östlichen Erweiterungsgebiete um die Piazza della Vittoria mit der Innenstadt verband.[17] Das Bogenmotiv der Tunneleinfahrt wurde genutzt, um es mit den rahmenden Doppeltürmen zu einem neuen, im Maßstab gesteigerten Stadttor auszuformulieren. [Abb. 6] 1932 lag die Planung für diesen Platz im Rahmen eines Regulierungsplanes für die Innenstadt vor. Der neue Platz war vor allem durch den Verkehr und den Handel geprägt, eine »Piazza spiccatamente di gran traffici, di smistamento, di intenso commercio«.[18] Dennoch spielte die künstlerisch-architektonische Fassung eine zentrale Rolle: »La piazza risultata appare quindi come la conveniente soluzione di vari problemi tecnici, studiata per costituire un raccordo facile al movimento, guidato dai detti assi obbligati, e risolvere pari tempo le complesse esigenze architettoniche di simmetria.«[19] Die erste Planung durch den Stadtingenieur Robaldo Morozzo della Rocca sah einen symmetrischen Platz vor, der von vier Hochhäusern an seinen Ecken gerahmt war. Der hinzugezogene Marcello Piacentini reduzierte die Anzahl der Türme auf zwei und schuf somit eine vermittelnde Abstufung zur Altstadt sowie das Motiv des Stadttores. Den südlichen der beiden Türme errichtete er zusammen mit dem Ingenieur Angelo Invernizzi 1935 – 40, der nördliche entstand 1935–37 nach den Plänen von Giuseppe Rosso. Geschickt sind die Hochbauten in eine Blockrandbebauung mit Normalhöhe eingebunden. Diese Blockrandbebauung fasst den Platz in gewohnten Proportionen und bietet mit ihren Arkaden auch den Fußgängern einen urbanen Raum. Die Hochhäuser markieren mit ihren Ecken exakt die Ecken des Platzes, treten mit ihren Breitseiten aber hinter der Blockrandbebauung in die zweite Reihe zurück. Geschickt ist mit diesem Kniff eine Überdominanz der Hochhauswände im Stadtraum vermieden, während die Eckansicht als dynamisierendes Element im Stadtraum hinzutritt.

Ganz von ihren städtebaulichen Wirkungen her waren die acht Hochhäuser konzipiert, die Stalin ab 1947 in Moskau errichten ließ.[20] Zum einen sollte die Silhouette der Welthauptstadt des Sozialismus neu akzentuiert

primarily by infrastructural and commercial elements, as a »piazza spiccatamente di gran traffico, di smistamento, di intenso comercio«.[18] Nevertheless, artistic and architectural features played a central role: »La piazza risultata appare quindi come la conveniente soluzione di vari problemi tecnici, studiata per costituire un raccordo facile al movimento, guidato dai detti assi obbligati, e risolvere pari tempo le complesse esigenze architettoniche di simmetria.«[19] The first plan by the city engineer Robaldo Morozzo della Rocca envisaged a symmetrical square, framed by four high-rise towers at its corners. Marcello Piacentini was consulted and he reduced the number of towers to two, thereby creating a mediating gradation towards the old city centre, as well as the motif of the city gate. He built the southern tower together with the engineer Angelo Invernizzi in 1935–40, while the northern one was built in 1935–37, according to designs by Giuseppe Rosso. The high structures are integrated cleverly into a perimeter development of a normal height. This perimeter development frames the square with its conventional proportions, while its arcades also provide pedestrians with an urban space. The corners of the high-rises mark the corners of the square exactly, but their broadsides are set back behind the perimeter development. This cleverly avoids an overdominance of the high-rise walls within the urban space, while the corner perspective adds a dynamic element to it.

The eight high-rises that Stalin built from 1947 in Moscow were conceived entirely from the point of view of their effect with the urban landscape.[20] First of all, the silhouette of the world capital of socialism was to be newly accentuated, so the high-rises were grouped in a ring around the planned Palace of the Soviets. Secondly, and this is of even greater interest in this context, the new high-rises were designed in relation to the public space that they were actually creating in the first place. A central aspect of the concept of the »multistory buildings« – the term »high-rise« was avoided consciously, so as not to evoke the capitalist class enemy in America – is that while they set their own accent within the cityscape, they nevertheless made references to the historic setting. The council of ministers had stipulated in January 1947:

d

werden – dazu wurden die Türme ringförmig um den geplanten Palast der Sowjets gruppiert. Zum anderen, und das ist in unserem Kontext interessanter, waren die neuen Hochhäuser in Zusammenhang mit dem öffentlichen Raum entworfen, den sie eigentlich erst schufen. Zentral war bei der Konzeption der »vielgeschossigen Gebäude« – der Terminus »Hochhaus« wurde bewusst gemieden, um nicht an den kapitalistischen Klassenfeind in Amerika zu erinnern –, dass sie zwar einen eigenen Akzent im Stadtbild setzten, jedoch an das historische Stadtbild anschlossen. So hatte der Ministerrat im Januar 1947 gefordert: »Die Proportionen und Umrisse dieser Gebäude müssen originell und in ihrer architektonisch-künstlerischen Komposition mit dem historisch gewachsenen architektonischen Bild der Stadt und mit der Silhouette des künftigen Palastes der Sowjets verbunden sein. In Übereinstimmung hiermit dürfen die zu projektierenden Gebäude nicht nach dem Muster bekannter vielgeschossiger Gebäude im Ausland gebaut sein.«[21]

Die 1947 verordneten acht Hochhausbauten fügten sich nahtlos in die Strategie des Moskauer Generalplans von 1935 ein.[22] Auch sie boten eine Fortsetzung der bestehenden Stadt mit traditionellen Mitteln, aber in neuen Dimensionen. Insbesondere die Silhouette der Stadt wurde nun mit an den alten Kirchtürmen orientierten Turmspitzen sozialistisch akzentuiert. Aber auch auf der Ebene des Stadtraums schufen die Hochhausbauten neue Stadtplätze, die vor allem Schlüsselstellen des Stadtplanes neu formulierten. Von den sieben ausgeführten Bauten ist einer in dieser Hinsicht besonders interessant.

Als Kopf eines ganzen Platzes war das Wohnhochhaus am Platz des Aufstands [heute Kudrinskaja-Platz] von Michail Posochin und Aschot Mindojanz [1949–54] angelegt. [Abb. 7] Dieser zum Gartenring ausgerichtete Platz sollte an beiden Seiten durch eine symmetrische zehngeschossige Blockrandbebebauung gefasst werden und mit einer geometrischen Bepflanzung zugleich einen städtischen Erholungsraum für die Anwohner bieten. Auch bei diesem Hochhaus tritt der eigentliche Turm vom Blockrand zurück, um noch einen zusätzlichen Vorhof auszubilden, der durch die sich abstufenden Flügel des ansonsten den Baublock ausfüllenden Hochhauses geformt wird. Mit seiner gleichförmigen Randbebauung und seiner Parkanlage nimmt der Platz des

e

»The proportions and outline of these buildings must be original and their architectural and artistic composition must refer to the historical architecture of the cityscape and to the silhouette of the future Palace of the Soviets. In accordance with this, the projected buildings must not be based on the models of famous multistory buildings in foreign countries.«[21]

The eight high-rise buildings decreed in 1947 were integrated seamlessly into the strategy of the Moscow general plan of 1935.[22] They also provided a continuation of the existing city, using traditional means, but in new dimensions. The silhouette of the city, in particular, was accentuated socialistically, with the tops of its towers reminiscent of old church towers. The high-rise buildings also created new urban squares in the context of the city, which reformulated key aspects of the city plan. Of all the buildings, one is particularly interesting in this respect.

The residential high-rise on Uprising Square [present-day Kudrinskaya Square], by Mikhail Posokhin and A. Mindoyants, was built as the head of the whole square in 1949–54 [Ill. 7]. This square, facing the garden ring, was to be lined on both sides by a symmetrical, ten-story perimeter development, providing an urban leisure area with geometrical vegetation for residents. The actual tower of this high-rise building is also set back from the perimeter, in order to create an additional front courtyard, formed by the tiered sides of the high building that otherwise fills the block. With its uniform perimeter development and its park area, Uprising Square adopts the tradition of the square, but lends it monumental proportions and a modern interpretation with its head-end, high-rise structure. The high-rise, as a new building type, has not only found its place within the city, but its new qualities have also created novel spaces within the city.

The history of urban development thus provides plenty of examples of the building of urban high-rise ensembles that incorporate urban squares. However, a quite different model has been at least equally significant: the utopia of high-speed transport links between high-rise agglomerations, as outlined around 1910 by the visionaries of a multistory New York, and then in 1914 by the futurist Antonio Sant'Elia in his ›città nuova‹. What appeared at the beginning of the twentieth cen-

Abb. 7
**Michail Posochin und Aschot Mindojanz,
Wohnhochhaus am Platz des Aufstands in Moskau, 1949–54**

Ill. 7
Michail Posochin and Aschot Mindojanz,
residential high-rise on the site of the uprising in Moscow,
1949–54

21
Rubanenko, B.:
»Die Architektur des Hochhauses am Kotelnitschesky-Ufer in Moskau«.
In: ›Deutsche Architektur‹.
H. 1, 1953, S. 28–34, hier S. 28

22
Oltarschewski, Wjatscheslaw:
›Stroitelstvo vysotnich zdanij w Moskwe‹
[Der Bau der Hochhäuser in Moskau].
Moskau 1953;
›Moskva – planirovka i zastrojka goroda
1945–1957‹ [Moskau – Planung und Bebauung der Stadt 1945–1957]. Moskau 1958

21
B. Rubanenko:
»Die Architektur des Hochhauses am Kotelnitschesky-Ufer in Moskau.«
In: ›Deutsche Architektur.‹
No. 1, 1953, pp. 28–34, here p. 28.

22
Wjatscheslaw Oltarschewski:
›Stroitelstvo vysotnich zdanij w Moskwe‹
[The Building of High-rises in Moscow].
Moscow 1953;
›Moskva – planirovka i zastrojka goroda
1945–1957‹ [Moscow – Planning and Building the City 1945–1957]. Moscow 1958.

d

Aufstands die Tradition des Square auf, die er aber mit neuen Dimensionen ins Monumentale steigert und mit einem als Hochhaus angelegten Kopfbau modern formuliert. Das Hochhaus hat als neuer Bautyp nicht allein seinen Platz in der Großstadt gefunden; es hat mit seinen neuen Qualitäten sogar neuartige Plätze in der Großstadt geschaffen.

Die Städtebaugeschichte bietet also reichlich Beispiele für die Anlage urbaner Hochhausensembles mit öffentlichen Plätzen. Doch mindestens ebenso folgenreich war ein ganz anderes Leitbild: die Utopie der rasanten Verkehrswege zwischen Hochhausgebirgen, wie sie um 1910 die Visionäre eines vielgeschossigen New York und dann 1914 der Futurist Antonio Sant' Elia in seiner »città nuova« gezeichnet hatten. Was zu Beginn des 20. Jahrhunderts von gesteigerter Urbanität imprägniert zu sein schien, erwies mit den Realisierungen der verkehrsgerechten Stadt sein wahres Gesicht: Die Reduzierung des öffentlichen Raums auf einen Raum des technisierten Verkehrs bedeutet die Zerstörung der Öffentlichkeit im Stadtraum. Die Unzulänglichkeit dieser Lösungen legt es nahe, wieder an die Tradition der städtebaulichen Einbindung des Hochhauses und der Verbindung von Hochhausbauten und Stadtplätzen in Ensembles anzuknüpfen. Hans Kollhoffs Entwurf für den Alexanderplatz in Berlin 1993 war dafür ein Meilenstein, und das Hochhausensemble von atelier ww und Max Dudler an der Thurgauerstrasse in Zürich-Oerlikon bildet dafür ein vorbildliches Beispiel.

e

tury to be the epitome of urbanity showed its true face when the reality of optimized infrastructure became evident: the reduction of public space to engineered infrastructural elements signifies the destruction of the public sphere within the city. The deficiencies and drawbacks of these solutions indicate that one should build on the tradition of integrating high-rises into the urban fabric, and of combining high-rise buildings and public spaces into ensembles. Hans Kollhoff's design for Alexanderplatz in Berlin in 1993 was a milestone in this respect, and the high-rise ensemble by atelier ww and Max Dudler on Thurgauerstrasse in Zurich-Oerlikon is a model example.

Blick vom Platz auf den Maintower an der Thurgauerstrasse
View from the square towards the Maintower on Thurgauerstrasse

Oben: Frühe Proportionsstudie, unten: Fassadendetails
Top: Early proportional study, bottom: Details of façades

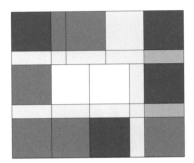 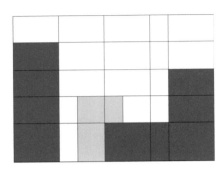

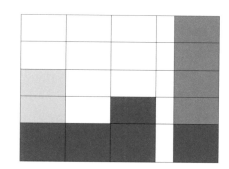

Oben: Frühe Proportionsstudie, unten: Fassadendetails
Top: Early proportional study, bottom: Details of façades

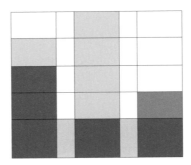

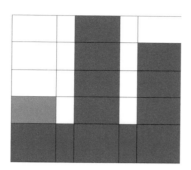

»Ich glaube auch Laien spüren das …«
Ein Gespräch mit Regula Lüscher
zur Quadroüberbauung

Alexander Bonte [AB] J. Christoph Bürkle [JCB]
Max Dudler für atelier ww architekten und Max Dudler [aww / MD]
Regula Lüscher, Senatsbaudirektorin Berlin [ehemals Zürich] [RL]

»I think non-experts notice it, too…«
A Discussion with Regula Lüscher
about the Quadro Development

Alexander Bonte [AB] J. Christoph Bürkle [JCB]
Max Dudler for atelier ww architekten and Max Dudler [aww / MD]
Regula Lüscher, Senate Building Director Berlin [previously Zürich] [RL]

d

e

JCB: 1984 wurde ein Hochhausverbot für die Zürcher Innenstadt durchgesetzt. 2000 begannen die Bauarbeiten am Doppelturm des Hochhausensembles. Regula Lüscher, heutige Senatsbaudirektorin von Berlin, hat mit dem Hochhausleitbild von 2001 seinerzeit in Zürich als Leiterin der Stadtplanung und stellvertretende Direktorin im Amt für Städtebau diesen Leitbildwechsel mitvollzogen. Wie kam es zu dieser Entwicklung?

RL: Weil es spürbar war, dass Zürich sich verdichtet und verdichten muss und weil wir überzeugt waren, dass das Hochhaus eine Möglichkeit ist, diesen Sprung in einen anderen Maßstab in dieser Stadt umzusetzen. Wir haben mit verschiedenen Stadtbaumeistern aus anderen Städten der Schweiz damals Gespräche geführt und intensiv darüber diskutiert. Es ging um das Hochhaus als Form der städtischen Verdichtung an zentralen, gut erschlossenen Standorten in der Stadt. Auch das Wohnen im Hochhaus war wieder Thema. Das war die Ausgangslage.

AB: Oerlikon war eine sehr heterogene Gegend. Auf dem Grundstück gab es einen Gebrauchthandel für Autos. Plötzlich präsentiert atelier ww dem damaligen Direktor des Amtes für Städtebau, Franz Eberhard, städtebauliche Ideen für Hochhäuser an dem Ort. Was war passiert? Das ist ja ein enormer Wachstumsschub!

RL: Damals war klar, dass Zürich-Nord der wichtigste Transformations- und Verdichtungsraum ist. Neben Zürich-West war das Entwicklungsgebiet Leutschenbach die Verbindungsstelle, die Nahtstelle in die Peripherie.

JCB: Die Hochhauskonzepte, die atelier ww für die Implenia entwickelt hatte, gaben dann den Anstoß zur städtischen Kooperativen Entwicklungsplanung Quartier Leutschenbach, das war 1998, und die Zusatzstudie Bahnhof Oerlikon Ost 2000. Was waren die städtebaulichen Leitbilder und gelten diese heute noch?

RL: Es herrschte die Überzeugung, dass in der Peripherie mehr innerstädtische Dichte und zusammenhängende Raumgefüge zu erzeugen seien. Oerlikon und Seebach war Peripherie, eine typische Agglomeration, von der man in der Schweiz so viele hat. Es ging zunächst um

JCB: In 1984, a prohibition on high-rise buildings in the city centre of Zurich was issued. The year 2000, however, saw the start of building work on the double tower of the high-rise ensemble. Regula Lüscher, the current Senate Building Director for Berlin, concurred with this change of principle at the time, as the then Director of Urban Planning and Deputy Director of the City Planning Office. How did this shift come about?

RL: It was evident that Zurich was experiencing a necessary densification, and we were of the opinion that high-rise buildings represent an option for realizing this expansion within the city. We held intense discussions with various urban planning experts from other Swiss cities at the time. We debated about high-rise buildings as a form of urban densification in central, easily accessible locations within the city, as well as the subject of living within high-rises. That was our starting point.

AB: Oerlikon was a very heterogeneous area. There was a second-hand car dealership on the site. Suddenly atelier ww presented the then Director of the City Planning Office, Franz Eberhard, with development ideas for high-rise buildings in this location. What had happened? It signified a huge expansion.

RL: At the time, it was clear that Zurich-Nord was the most important transformation and densification area. The Leutschenbach development area, next to Zurich-West, was the connection point, the interface in the periphery.

JCB: The high-rise concepts that atelier ww developed together with Implenia provided the impetus back in 1998 for the Leutschenbach Quarter cooperative urban development plan, and for the supplementary study of the Oerlikon East train station in 2000. What were the urban development principles and are these still valid today?

RL: It was believed that it was possible to create a greater urban density and more coherent spatial ensembles in the periphery. Oerlikon and Seebach was in

Zwischenbauzustand:
Doppelturm ohne zweite Bauetappe
Construction in progress:
double tower before the second building stage

d

Dichte und eine klarere Differenzierung zwischen öffentlichem und privatem Raum. Öffentlicher Raum sollte geschaffen und bestehender aufgewertet werden. Das zeigt sich etwa an der Schaffung des zentralen Parks oder Platzes von Leutschenbach. Der ist beides: Platz und Park – eine Art Zwischending. Die Erinnerung an das Wettbewerbsverfahren für den Platz ist mir noch sehr präsent. In der Jury haben wir intensiv und konträr darüber diskutiert, ob und wie stark Bilder des klassischen Städtebaus durch den Entwurf an diesem Ort neu entstehen sollen.

AB: Bei den Neubauten an der Europaallee in Zürich spricht man von einer »Neuen Dichte«, sie folgen der Strategie einer Verdichtung nach innen. In Zürich-West erkennt man einen »Assimilationsprozess«, in dessen Rahmen die vorhandenen Bauten des ehemaligen Industriequartiers in die kontinuierliche, städtische Raumabfolge eingegliedert werden. In Zürich-Nord könnte man eine dritte Strategie ausmachen, die der urbanen Inseln. Der Architekt Mario Campi hat Zürich-Nord in dem Buch ›Annähernd perfekte Peripherie‹ als Mosaik oder als Flickenteppich bezeichnet.

RL: Ja, das war wohl die Vision. Es ging nicht darum, perfekte innerstädtische Verhältnisse zu inszenieren, weil eigentlich alle wussten, dass das, was an Architektur schon dort ist, sich nicht so schnell verändern wird und dass man mit Einbezug des Bestandes neue Stadträume und eine neue Stadttypologie entwickeln muss. Die bestehenden urbanen Inseln in Leutschenbach hatten nicht die architektonische Substanz wie die in Zürich-West, die sehr identitätsstiftend sind.

JCB: Mittlerweile wirken die vier Hochhäuser wie ein Tor zu Leutschenbach. Es wurde seitdem und wird noch viel gebaut. Aber wie hat es begonnen, welches Leitbild hat man mit den Hochhäusern umsetzen wollen?

RL: Da muss ich eingreifen! Das Ensemble ist überhaupt nicht das Resultat einer übergeordneten Planung. Diese Stadtvorstellung, die hier entstanden ist, das ist eine Insel, und das ist einfach atelier ww und Max Dudler.

JCB: Und das war auch so geplant?

e

the periphery, a typical agglomeration of which there are so many in Switzerland. It was primarily about densification and a clearer differentiation between public and private space. The aim was to create additional public space and to upgrade the public space that was already there, as can be seen by the establishment of the central park or of the Leutschenbach square, which is both: a square and a park – a kind of hybrid. I still clearly remember the competition procedure for the square. Within the jury, we discussed intensely and controversially about whether and to what extent traditional visions of urban development were to be emulated by the plans for this location.

AB: With regard to the new buildings on Europaallee in Zurich, there is talk of a »new density«, following a strategy of inward densification. In Zurich-West one can identify an »assimilation process«, whereby the existing buildings in the former industrial district are integrated into the continuous urban sequence of spaces. In Zurich-Nord one can make out a third strategy, namely that of urban islands. The architect Mario Campi described Zurich-Nord as a mosaic or patchwork rug in his book ›Annähernd perfekte Peripherie‹ [»An almost perfect periphery«].

RL: Yes, I suppose that was the vision. It was not about setting up new and perfect inner-city environments, because actually everyone knew that the architecture that was already there would not change very quickly or disappear and that it was necessary to develop new urban spaces and a new urban typology that incorporated the existing buildings and structures. The existing urban islands in Leutschenbach did not have the architectural substance of those in Zurich-West, which are very distinctive.

JCB: Now the four high-rise buildings appear as a gateway to Leutschenbach. There has been and continues to be lot of building since then. But how did it start, and what were the principles behind the high-rise ensemble?

RL: I have to intervene here! The ensemble was not at all dictated by a superordinate plan. The urban con-

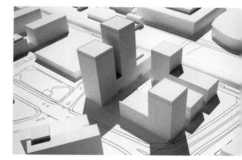

Städtebauliches Modell
Urban development model

Schnittdarstellung aus dem Architekturwettbewerb
Cross-sectional view from the architecture competition

d

RL: Nein, das war überhaupt nicht so geplant. Es war Resultat eines diskursiven Verfahrens und nicht einer übergeordneten Planung aus der Verwaltung. Ich habe diesen Ort immer als Insel gelesen, und diese hochverdichtete, extrem urbane Insel wurde in der Leutschenbachplanung nicht weitergeführt, das war nicht das Vorbild, das sind zwei unterschiedliche Welten. In diesem Sinne ist es auch heute noch eine etwas irritierende, fremde Insel. Ich empfinde es auf jeden Fall so.

aww/MD: Franz Eberhard, der damalige Direktor des Amtes für Städtebau, war von der Hochhausidee angetan, aber er wollte einen Wettbewerb. Anstelle eines Wettbewerbs wurde aber schließlich ein diskursives Verfahren mit der Arge atelier ww / Max Dudler und der Stadt Zürich gewählt, weil das Vorteile für die Architekten gegenüber der Bauherrschaft verspricht.

RL: Genau, so war es. Die Hochhäuser sind also nicht das Resultat einer gewollten Planung, als ob die Stadt Zürich an dieser Stelle zwei Hochhäuser vorgesehen hätte, sondern das Vorhaben war eine private Grundstücksentwicklung. diAx wollte zunächst zwei signifikante Türme und nichts anderes.

aww/MD: Und es kam der zukünftige Stadtpräsident, Elmar Ledergerber, der wollte die diAx unbedingt in der Stadt halten. Wir haben dann mit Frau Lüscher ein diskursives Verfahren gestartet. Man traf sich alle zwei Wochen am runden Tisch. Zusammen haben wir dann die diAx Tower entwickelt. Die zweite Etappe wurde erst durch den Entschluss der Amag möglich, mit dem Autooccasionshandel auszuziehen. Diesmal wurde ein hochkarätig besetzter internationaler Wettbewerb ausgeschrieben, bei dem sich die Arge erfolgreich durchsetzen konnte. Vielleicht weil wir von Anfang an ein Ensemble vorgeschlagen hatten, eine Stadt in der Stadt innerhalb von Leutschenbach. Wir haben damals an amerikanische Zentren wie das Rockefeller-Center gedacht.

RL: Ich finde es übrigens nicht mal so schlimm, dass das Zentrum so etwas wie eine »autistische Insel« geworden ist, dadurch passt es wiederum zum Kontext.

e

cept that emerged here is an island, that of atelier ww and Max Dudler.

JCB: And was it planned as such?

RL: No, it was not planned like that at all. It was the result of a discursive process, and not of planning by the municipal authorities. I have always viewed this site as an island, and this very dense, extremely urban island was not replicated in the further planning for Leutschenbach. It was not a model, instead there were two different worlds alongside each other. In this respect, still today it is a rather conspicuous, alien island. At least that's how I view it.

aww/MD: Franz Eberhard, the then Director of the City Planning Office, was enthused by the high-rise idea, but he wanted a competition. However, instead of a competition, he finally opted for a discursive process with the work group atelier ww / Max Dudler and the city of Zurich, because it promised advantages for the architects as opposed to the developers.

RL: Yes, that's right, that's how it was. So the high-rise buildings are not the result of intentional planning, in the sense of the municipality of Zurich wanting to have two high-rise buildings on this site. Instead, the project was a private develoment. DiAx initially wanted two significant towers and nothing else.

aww/MD: And then the future city governor, Elmar Ledergerber, came along and he wanted to keep the DiAx within the city. Then we started a discursive process with Ms. Lüscher. We met every two weeks at the round table and developed the DiAx tower concept together. The second stage was enabled by Amag's decision to move the car dealership off the site. This time a high-level international competition was held, which the work group won, perhaps because we had proposed an ensemble from the beginning, a city within the city in Leutschenbach. At the time we were thinking of American centers such as Rockefeller Center.

RL: In fact, I don't think it is such a bad thing that the

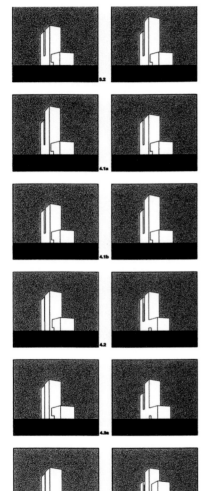

**Baukörperstudien zum
Doppelturm der ersten Etappe**
Structural studies of the
double tower in the first phase

d

aww/MD: Ja, auch gegenüber der Messe, die ja selbst so eine Insel ist. Die Quadroüberbauung ist ein Ensemble, wie das schon erwähnte Rockefeller-Center. Sehr stark verdichtet. Es sind vier Gebäude mit dem gleichen Stein, dem gleichen Fensterformat, ein Stück Stadt mit einem zentralen Platz. Vielleicht muss man dem Platz noch fünf Jahre geben, bis er richtig belebt ist. Trotzdem ist es richtig, an der Peripherie oder der Zwischenstadt ein solches Zeichen zu setzen, das sich vielleicht erst mit der Zeit mit dem Umfeld verbinden wird.

JCB: Wird die Wirkung nicht noch stärker, wenn das Ensemble irgendwann besser in das Umfeld eingebunden wird? Kann man das planerisch überhaupt steuern?

RL: Städtebau und Stadtentwicklung ist das Pragmatischste, was man sich vorstellen kann. Die Stärke dieser Hochhäuser in Oerlikon liegt darin, dass sie bereits als Ensemble funktionieren, auch wenn noch lange Zeit rundherum Autofirmen da stehen werden, und dass es die Kraft hat, einen urbanen Verbindungspunkt zwischen Leutschenbach – das sich tatsächlich etwas urbaner entwickelt – und dem Bahnhof Oerlikon zu bilden. Es wird aber auch noch in 100 Jahren hervorragend funktionieren, wenn das Leutschenbachquartier verdichtetste Innenstadt sein wird. Das Faszinierende ist ja, dass wir permanent über die Peripherie nachdenken und uns überlegen müssen: »Was sind die richtigen Strategien in der Peripherie?« Und dass wir hier eine Strategie haben, die zunächst absolut innerstädtisch ist, absolut fremd und erst mal verfehlt, dass sie aber, weil sie gut gemacht ist, immer perfekt funktioniert. Die Antwort auf die Frage: »Was ist Stadt?« verändert sich gerade hier permanent und das ist hochspannend. Das freut mich jedes Mal, wenn ich daran vorbeifahre, ich glaube, auch Laien spüren das …

aww/MD: Ja, ich glaube die Leute merken das langsam. Bei der Eröffnung war eine ältere Dame, die aus dem Büro herauskam und meinte: »Da fühlen wir uns wie in New York« … [alle lachen]
Wir haben auch vorgeschlagen, im Winter einen Eisplatz zu installieren, damit die unterschiedlichsten Leute kommen. Es gibt jetzt schon viele Restaurants in der Umgebung, aber all das braucht viel Zeit, genauso

e

center has become something of an »autistic island«, as it fits within its context.

aww/MD: Yes, and it is opposite the trade fair, which itself is such an island. The Quadro development is an ensemble like the mentioned Rockefeller Center, with a high density. It comprises four buildings made of the same stone, with the same window format. It is a piece of the city with a central square. Perhaps we have to give the square another five years before it truly comes to life. Even so, it is right to set such an example in the periphery or in-between area of the city, which might take time to integrate itself with its surroundings.

JCB: Won't the impact be even greater when the ensemble has been integrated better into its surroundings? Can this actually be controlled from a planning point of view?

RL: There is nothing more pragmatic than urban construction and development. The strength of these high-rise buildings in Oerlikon lies in the fact that they already function as an ensemble, even if it will still be surrounded by car companies for a long time, and that its strong presence forms an urban connection point between Leutschenbach – which is in fact experiencing a more urban development – and the Oerlikon train station. It will still function wonderfully in a hundred years, when the Leutschenbach quarter has become a very dense inner-city district. What is fascinating is that we are constantly thinking about the periphery and have to consider: »What are the right strategies in the periphery?«, and that we have a strategy here that is primarily urban and absolutely alien, but which functions perfectly because it is well thought out. The answer to the question: »What is a city?« is experiencing a permanent and very interesting shift here. I am struck by it every time I drive past it, and I think non-experts notice it, too…

aww/MD: Yes, we think people are gradually becoming aware of it. At the opening there was an older lady who came of the office and said: »There it feels like we're in New York«… [everyone laughs]

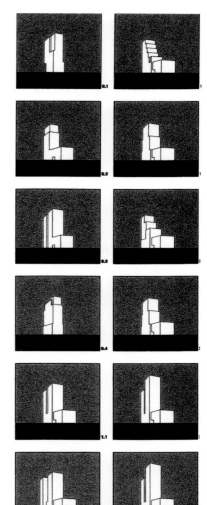

Baukörperstudien zum Doppelturm der ersten Etappe
Structural studies of the double tower in the first phase

d

wie in der Europaallee. Auch der Europaallee müssen wir Zeit geben, bis sich das Quartier mit Leben füllt und die Bürger die neue Umgebung angenommen haben.

Mit der »Grünstadt Zürich« gab es viele Sitzungen zur Gestaltung des Platzes. Und es ist wichtig, dass es diesen öffentlichen Platz gibt, der rundherum mit öffentlichen Einrichtungen bespielt ist. Dazu zählen auch die Arkaden, unter denen man geschützt um den Platz rumlaufen kann. Solche erprobten Typologien sind wichtig für die Stadt.

JCB: Das Ensemble ist ja fast schon ein Stadtzeichen, das man von überall her wahrnimmt. Man weiß gleich, wo man ist. Wie plant man so etwas? Oder entsteht diese Zeichenhaftigkeit auch ein wenig per Zufall?

aww/MD: Also entschuldigen Sie Herr Bürkle, Architektur ist nie Zufall …

JCB: Also ist das Ensemble doch ein Ergebnis der Planung?

RL: Es ist eben beides! Die Geschichte des Projekts beginnt für die Stadt damit, dass einer kommt, der einen Turm bauen will. Und dann überlegt man sich: »Hm, was löst das aus, passt das, funktioniert das?« Unsere Aufgabe besteht darin, herauszufinden: »Wie kann es funktionieren, dass es wirklich zu einem Mehrwert führt?« Und so kommt es zu einer Entwicklung, die hier damit endet, dass ein Hochhausensemble um einen öffentlichen Platz geschaffen wurde.

Und der Platz wird am Schluss eigentlich das Herzstück – und nicht die Tatsache, dass dort ein Hochhaus stehen sollte. Das ist prozessuale Planung, das ist Auseinandersetzung. Das geht nur, wenn man sich bewusst ist, dass man jede Idee qualifizieren muss. Das war auch der Grund, warum wir den Wettbewerb durchgeführt haben. Ja, Planung muss beides können; vorgeben und loslassen. Darum sage ich: Stadtplanung ist manchmal wahnsinnig pragmatisch. Stadtplanung funktioniert eigentlich so, dass man permanent die Veränderungen steuern muss. Man muss die Energie der Veränderung in die richtige Richtung steuern. Dafür sind dann letztlich die Senatsbaudirektorinnen und

e

We also suggested installing an ice rink in winter, to attract a wide range of people. There are already many restaurants in the area, but all of this takes a lot of time, just like on Europaallee. We also have to give Europaallee time for it to fill up with life and for residents to accept the new environment.

In the end, it was the municipality that insisted on a real square being created here, a public space that could be experienced. There were many meetings to discuss the design of the square, as part of »Green City Zurich«. This public square, which has public amenities all around it, plays an important role. This includes the arcades, which provide shelter when wandering around the square. Such well-tried typologies are important for the city.

JCB: The ensemble is almost already a city landmark, which can be seen from all directions. You know immediately where you are. How does one plan this? Or is this emblematic character also somewhat coincidental?

aww/MD: Excuse me, Mr. Bürkle, but architecture is never coincidental…

JCB: So the ensemble is in fact a result of planning then?

RL: Well, it is both! The story of the project began with someone coming and wanting to build a tower. This prompted further considerations: »Hm, what impact will that have, does it fit, does it work?« Our task was to find out: »How can it work, so that it really brings added value to the area?« This resulted in a development that saw a high-rise ensemble being built around a public square.

And the square ultimately became the actual centerpiece – rather than the fact that high-rise buildings were to be built there. It was a case of procedural planning, which is only possible if one is aware that one has to qualify every idea. This was also the reason we held the competition. Yes, planning has to be able to do both: to specify and to let go. That's why I say: urban planning can be extremely pragmatic. The way urban planning works is by continuously direct-

d

Stadtbaumeister da. Es ist ihr Job, das Potenzial zu erkennen, das einem Projekt zugrunde liegt, um daraus etwas zu machen.

AB: Der Planungsprozess hat über 15 Jahre gedauert. Doch das Endergebnis ist nahezu deckungsgleich mit dem Wettbewerbsprojekt. Das ist erstaunlich. Zieht man den Vergleich zur stockenden Planung am Alexanderplatz in Berlin, dann fragt man sich, ob das vielleicht an der präzisen Architektur der Quadroüberbauung liegt.

RL: Ich glaube, dass die Unterschiede zwischen Zürich und Berlin woanders zu suchen sind. Es liegt daran, dass die Planung in Zürich erst vorangetrieben wurde, als auch parallel ein Wirtschaftsdruck da war. Der Kollhoff-Plan war über Jahrzehnte nicht umsetzbar, weil eine viel zu geringe Wirtschaftskraft dahinterstand. Kollhoff hat eine architektonische Setzung gemacht und nicht einen Masterplan. Dies entspricht seiner baulichen Haltung. Es ist ein viel zu großes zusammenhängendes architektonisches Projekt, das nur funktioniert, wenn es aus einer Hand und in überschaubarer Zeit realisiert wird – was eine völlige Illusion ist. In einem kleineren Maßstab, wie hier in Zürich, funktioniert eine Strategie, die Architektur und Städtebau als Einheit begreift und wo die Qualität des Städtebaus mit der architektonischen Stringenz gekoppelt wird. Sobald man sich in einem größeren Maßstab befindet, wie zum Beispiel am Alexanderplatz in Berlin, braucht es andere Strategien, die flexibler sind. Es ist eine Illusion zu glauben, dass wir zehn Investoren finden, die alle den gleichen Turm bauen wollen. Im Gegenteil: Jeder will sein Unikat, sonst bauen sie gar keine Hochhäuser. Und das war das Starke hier: Die beiden Türme, die waren gebaut. Und nachher kam das Ensemble dazu.

aww/MD: Gottlob, es wäre eine Katastrophe für das gesamte Gebiet gewesen, wenn der Doppelturm allein geblieben wäre. Das Zeitlose und die Stringenz, von der Sie, Frau Lüscher, gesprochen haben, wären dann nicht gegeben. Auch die Anschlussfähigkeit des Quartiers, die Möglichkeit des Weiterbauens wäre eine ganz andere. Städtebau kann heute nur noch so funktionieren: Es entsteht ein Stück Stadt und das strahlt dann aus und verbindet sich irgendwann mit der alten Stadt.

e

ing the changes. One has to guide the energy of change in the right direction. This is what the Senate Building Directors and urban planning authorities are ultimately there for. It is their job to identify the potential harboured by a project and to make something of it.

AB: The planning process lasted over fifteen years, but the end result is practically the same as the competition project. That is astounding. If you compare it to the long-drawn-out planning of Alexanderplatz in Berlin, then you wonder whether this is perhaps because of the specific architecture of the Quadro development.

RL: I believe that the reasons for the differences between Zurich and Berlin lie elsewhere. It is because the planning in Zurich was only driven forwards when there was also economic pressure. The Kollhoff plan could not be realized for decades, because there was much too little economic power behind it. Kollhoff put forward an architectural proposal and not a master plan. It was a coherent, much too large-scale architectural project, which would only work if it was built by one party and within a manageable timeframe – which is a complete illusion. On a smaller scale, like here in Zurich, the only viable strategy is one that understands architecture and urban development as an entitiy, and which couples the quality of urban development with architectural stringency. On a larger scale, as for example Alexanderplatz in Berlin, one needs other strategies that are more flexible. It is an illusion to believe that we will find ten investors who all want to build the same tower. On the contrary: everyone wants their own unique building, or none at all. And this was the advantage in this case: the two towers were already built and the ensemble was added later.

aww/MD: Thank goodness, it would have been a disaster for the whole district if the double tower had remained on its own. Then it would not have had the timelessness and the stringency that you spoke about, Ms. Lüscher, and it would not have had the same potential to connect the district and develop it further.

d

Und so kann Städtebau auch in der Peripherie funktionieren. Stadt wie im 19. Jahrhundert, das ist vorbei.

AB: Ich möchte noch einmal auf die Architektur in der Peripherie zu sprechen kommen. Rem Koolhaas sagt, der Grundmodul der »Generic City«, wie er es nennt, wäre der Desktop-Computer, darauf könne man alles aufbauen. Das trifft auch auf das Hochhausensemble zu. Die Architektur ist sehr typologisch entworfen worden. Doch die Architektur ist nicht einfach nur rational; alles ist ganz einfach und präzise, doch in der Stadt wird das Ensemble zu einem Zeichen, zu einem Emblem. Das ist, meine ich, das Interessante an der Architektur, besonders im Bezug zur Peripherie.

aww/MD: Ja, die Architektur wird durch Wiederholung und durch skulpturale Qualitäten, die ganz präzise gesetzt sind, geprägt. Wenn man Grundriss und Aufriss nach einem Prinzip entwickelt, das eine gewisse Qualität und Aussagekraft hat, dann wird dieses Prinzip irgendwann sinnlich. Das kann man hier sehen: Architektur hat mit Licht und Schatten zu tun, die europäische Stadt mit Plätzen, Arkaden und Gassen, und plötzlich lebt das Ensemble als Ganzes. Zugleich geht es auch um das Repetitive in der Stadt. Unsere Baukörper sind fast ähnlich, sie sind nicht gleich, sie haben immer eine leicht andere Ausformulierung. Diese Architektur spricht eine zeitlose Sprache, und führt, wenn sie gut ist, zu etwas Sinnlichem. Wenn die Menschen das einmal angenommen haben, wie wir es vorhin gesagt haben, dann wird dieses Stück Stadt immer Qualität haben.

JCB: Also für mich ist das Ensemble eher ein Manifest des Rationalismus. Wenn ich dort auf dem Platz an den Arkaden stehe, dann fühle ich mich an Bilder von Giorgio de Chirico erinnert, wenn es dann noch Schlagschatten gibt …

aww/MD: Stärker als die Bilder hat uns das darin vermittelte Prinzip interessiert: Räumlichkeit, Typologie, Materialität. Ob das nun rational ist oder nicht, müssen sie entscheiden. Die Wiederholung endet nicht in der Langeweile, sondern in der Sinnlichkeit, in einer Art Kunstform.

e

Urban development can only work like this nowadays: a piece of the city is created, which radiates outwards and at some point interconnects with the old city. This is also how urban development can work in the periphery. Cities as they were in the nineteenth century are a thing of the past.

AB: I would like to come back to architecture in the periphery. Rem Koolhaas says that the basic module of the »Generic City«, as he calls it, is the desktop computer, which everything can be built up on. This also applies to the high-rise ensemble. The architecture has been designed very typologically. However, it is not merely rational, with everything simple and precise. Within the city, the ensemble also appears as a landmark, an emblem. I think this is what is interesting about the architecture, especially in relation to the periphery.

aww/MD: Yes, the architecture is characterized by repetition and sculptural qualities, which are positioned very precisely. If you develop a layout and elevation according to a principle that promotes a certain quality and expressive power, then at some point this principle gains a sensual aspect. You can see that in this case: architecture involves light and shade, the European city with its squares, arcades, and alleys, and suddenly the ensemble emerges as a whole. At the same time it is also about repetitive elements within the city. Our buildings are similar, but they are not the same. They always have a slightly different formulation. This architecture speaks a timeless language and gains, if it is good, a sensual aspect. Once the people have accepted it, as we said before, this part of the city will always have a certain quality.

JCB: Well, in my opinion the ensemble is more like a manifestation of rationalism. When I am standing by the arcades on the square there, it calls to mind paintings by Giorgio de Chirico, especially if there are cast shadows…

aww/MD: What interested us more than these images was the principle they conveyed: spatiality, typology, materiality. It is up to you to decide whether that is

Zwischenstand aus der Planung:
Das Stadthaus mit großer Stadtloggia im Erdgeschoss
Intermediate planning state:
the townhouse with a large loggia on the ground floor

d

JCB: Es ist diese starke Großform, die es in Zürich kaum gibt.

aww/MD: Doch, doch, es gibt die kantonale Verwaltung oder die Häuser an der Walche, von den Gebrüdern Pfister gebaut. Das ist eines der interessantesten Gebäudeensembles aus den 1930er Jahren, das sich sehr gut in die Stadt einfügt. Also es gibt schon Vorbilder, auch in Zürich.

JCB: Man könnte es auch andersherum interpretieren, nämlich dass die Gebäude für Oerlikon fast zu stark sind. Dass die Wirkung so mächtig ist, dass sie das Umfeld gleichsam erstarren lässt.

RL: Ja, das erlebe ich auch so. Aber das ist genau die Stärke. Gerade die Tatsache, dass das Ensemble und seine fast brachiale städtische Eleganz an der Stelle durchaus befremdlich wirken. An der Walche ist Zürich ja auch mal so richtig städtisch, sodass man beinahe erschrickt. In einer gewissen Art und Weise sind die Hochhäuser unzürcherisch. Und sie haben erst mal gar nichts mit Peripherie zu tun. Aber sie haben eben umgekehrt wieder extrem viel mit Peripherie zu tun, weil sie zusammen eine kompakte Inselgruppe bilden, frei im fließenden Raum der Peripherie. Als geschlossenes Ensemble sind sie ebenso Solitär wie das Hallenstadion nebenan. Das ist für mich das Faszinierende.

JCB: Im Rückblick die obligate Frage: Würde man heute etwas anders machen?

aww/MD: Wir nicht.

RL: Nein.

JCB: Super!

e

rational or not. The repetition does not become tedious, but sensual, a kind of art form.

JCB: There are few such imposing, large forms in Zurich.

aww/MD: But there are, such as the cantonal administration or the houses by the Walche, built by the Pfister brothers. That is one of the most interesting building ensembles from the nineteen-thirties, which is well integrated into the city. So there are actually some models, even in Zurich.

JCB: It can also be interpreted the other way round, namely that the buildings are almost too imposing for Oerlikon, that their impact is so great that it neutralizes the surroundings.

RL: Yes, that's how I see it too. But precisely that is their strength. The fact that the ensemble and its almost brute urban elegance appear rather outlandish on this site. Zurich can be almost alarmingly urban by the Walche. In a way, the high-rise buildings are untypical of Zurich, and they are not what one would expect in the periphery in the first instance. However, on the other hand they are very fitting within the periphery, because together they form a compact insular group, free-standing within the flowing space of the periphery. As a closed ensemble, therefore, they are just as much a solitaire as the adjacent Hallenstadion events venue. That is what I find fascinating.

JCB: The obligatory question in retrospect is: would you do anything differently today?

aww/MD: We wouldn't, no.

RL: No.

JCB: Great!

Regula Lüscher

Pläne
Plans

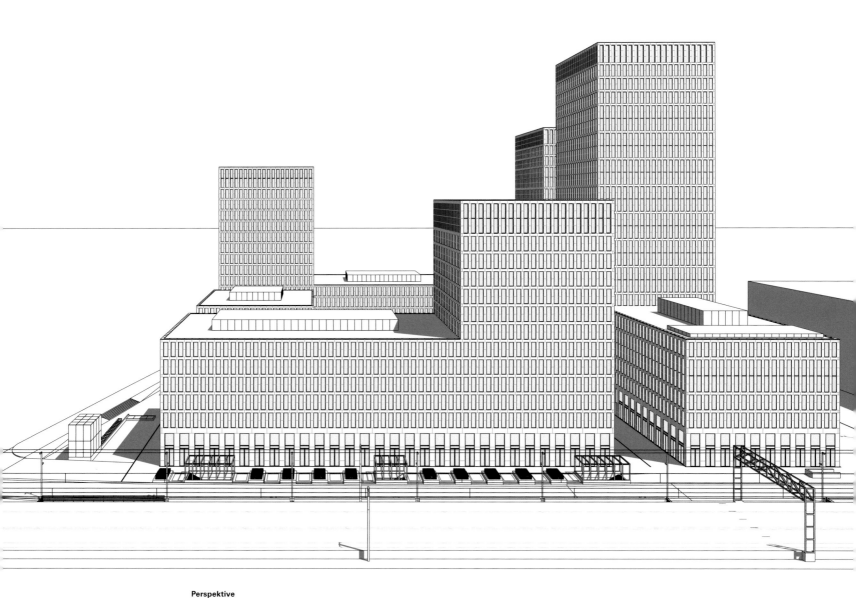

Perspektive
Perspective

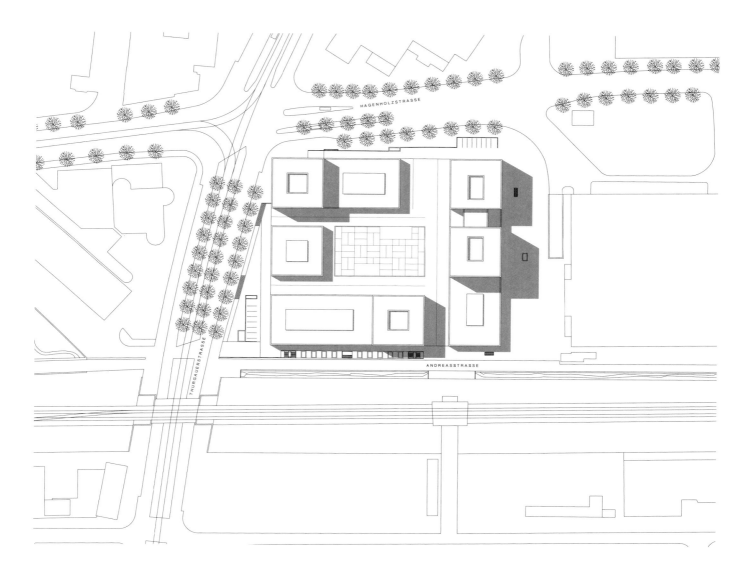

Situationsplan
Site plan

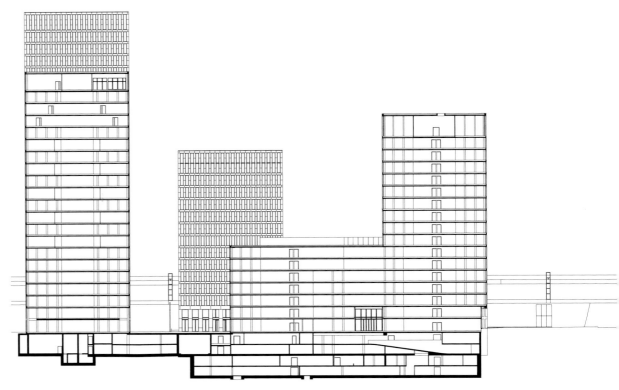

Schnitt Ost-West Richtung Süd
East-west cross section facing South

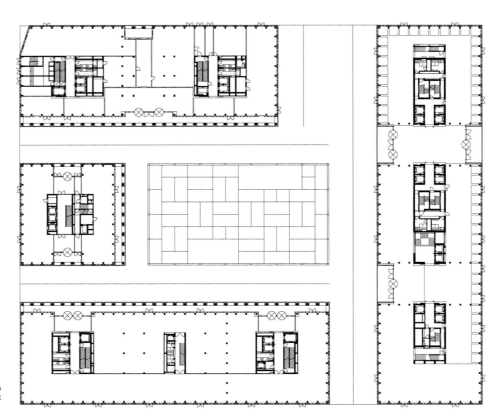

Grundriss Erdgeschoss
Ground floor layout

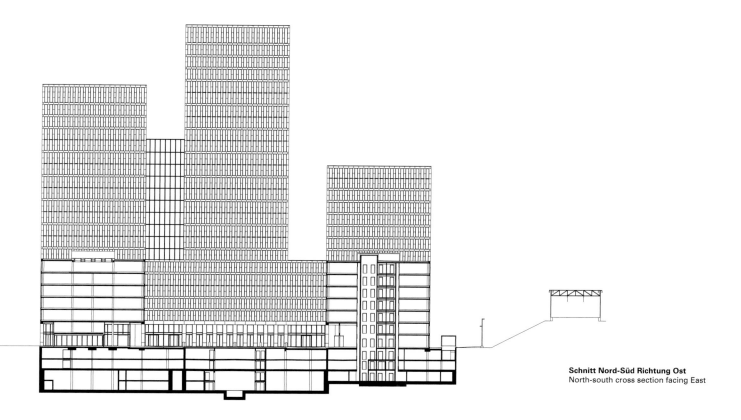

Schnitt Nord-Süd Richtung Ost
North-south cross section facing East

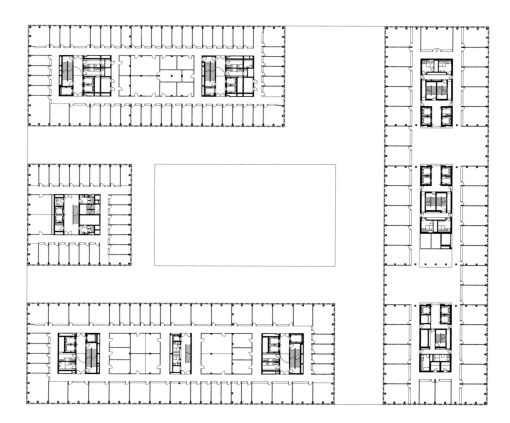

Grundriss Regelgeschoss Sockel
Layout of standard base level

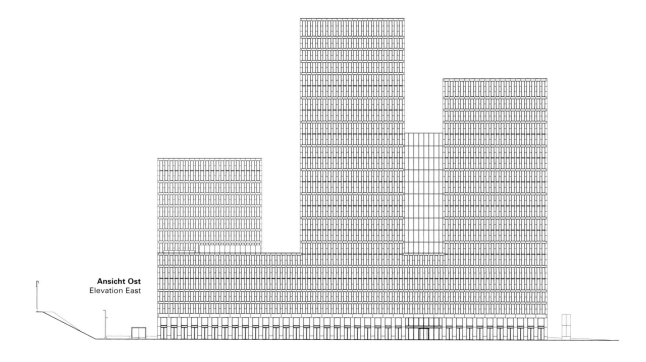

Ansicht Ost
Elevation East

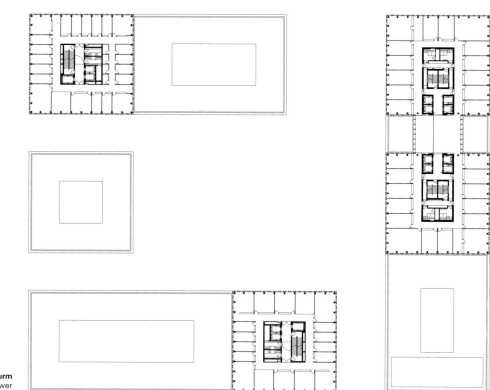

Grundriss Regelgeschoss Turm
Layout of standard tower

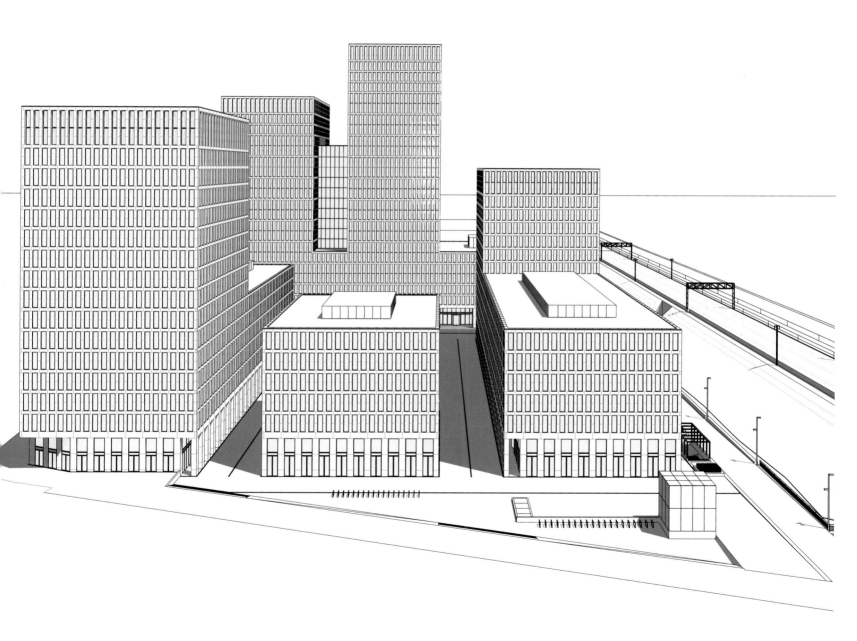

Perspektive
Perspective

Index zum
Hochhausensemble Thurgauerstrasse

Alexander Bonte

Index for the
High-rise Ensemble on Thurgauerstrasse

Alexander Bonte

**Urs Wüst und/and Walter Wäschle
atelier ww Architekten SIA AG**

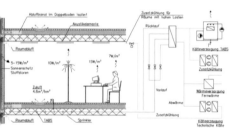

Energiekonzept
Energy concept

d

Adresse
Hagenholzstrasse 20 / 22 / Andreasstrasse / Thurgauerstrasse 30 / 32 / 34 / 36 / 38,
CH-8050 Zürich

atelier ww Architekten SIA AG
Walter Wäschle ist zusammen mit Urs und Rolf Wüst Inhaber des 1970 in
Zürich gegründeten atelier ww. Walter Wäschle diplomierte an der Akademie
der bildenden Künste in Wien, Urs Wüst an der Akademie der bildenden Kün-
ste in Düsseldorf.
Die Arbeiten des atelier ww umfassen alle Bereiche des Städtebaus und der
Architektur. Viele Projekte resultieren aus gewonnenen Wettbewerben. Das
Portfolio umfasst ein breites Spektrum an Bauten mit unterschiedlichsten Nut-
zungen und Volumen wie Messebauten, Einkaufszentren, Hotels, Büro- und
Gewerbebauten sowie Industrie- und Wohnbauten.

Bauherr
BVK Personalvorsorge des Kantons Zürich [»CS-Towers« und »Vertex«]. Die BVK
ist die Vorsorgeeinrichtung für die Angestellten des Kantons Zürich, die größte
Pensionskasse der Schweiz.
AXA Leben AG vertreten durch AXA Investment Managers Schweiz AG [»Main-
tower«]. Beide Unternehmen sind Teile der AXA-Gruppe, die zu den führenden
Assetmanagern weltweit zählt.

Baukörper / Kenndaten
Das Grundstück an der Thurgauerstrasse hat eine Fläche von 15.421 Quadratmetern, auf der die Bebauung über einem Feld von 103,2 Metern x 119,4 Metern
aufgeht. Das Ensemble besteht aus vier Baukörpern, die sich um einen zentralen Binnenplatz, den Quadroplatz, gruppieren: den Doppelturm [CS] im Osten,
das nördliche Hochhaus [Maintower/ AXA], das südliche Hochhaus [Geschäfts-
haus/ BVK] und das westlich dazwischen angeordnete kleinere Stadthaus
[Stadthaus/ BVK]. Alle vier Häuser weisen eine Sockelbebauung von 23,70
Metern Höhe / sieben Geschossen auf, darüber erheben sich vier Hochhäuser
mit 88 Metern / 21 Geschossen zw. 72,50 Metern / 26 Geschossen [CS], 59,50
Metern / 17 Geschossen [AXA] und 49,60 Metern / 14 Geschossen [BVK]. Die
Regelgeschosshöhe im Ensemble beträgt 3,30 Meter, im Erdgeschoss 3,80
Meter. Das Gesamtbauvolumen umfasst insgesamt 136.500 Quadratmeter
Geschossfläche [GF] / 474.400 Kubikmeter Gebäudevolumen [GV]; davon entfallen 60.000 Quadratmeter GF / 215.000 Kubikmeter GV auf den Bauteil CS,
31.300 Quadratmeter GF / 16.740 Kubikmeter GV auf den Bauteil AXA und
31.300 Quadratmeter GF / 106.800 Kubikmeter GV auf das Geschäftshaus BVK
und 13.900 Quadratmeter GF / 45.950 Kubikmeter auf das Stadthaus BVK.

Energiekonzept
Durch die intelligente Integration von Fassade, Tragkonstruktion und technischer Gebäudeausrüstung wurde für alle Häuser des Ensembles ein modernes,
umweltfreundliches Energiekonzept realisiert, das mit dem Minergie-Zertifikat
ausgezeichnet wurde. Drei Elemente bilden die Hauptmerkmale des zugleich
platzsparenden, ökologischen und wirtschaftlichen Energiekonzeptes: Die Abluftfassade mit Sonnenschutz im Scheibenzwischenraum, das thermoaktive
Bauteilsystem [TABS] zum Heizen und Kühlen in den Stahlbetondecken und
eine effiziente Quelllufteinführung über die Doppelböden der Bürobereiche. Auf
diese Weise wird eine optimale Raumkonditionierung mit hohem Raumkomfort
bei moderaten Energiekosten und günstigem Investitionsaufwand erreicht.
Bezogen auf den einzelnen Raum passiert dabei folgendes: Die Zuluft wird
zentral aufbereitet und über Bodenluftdurchlässe laminar in die Räume geführt. Über die Abluftfassade wird die Luft an der Decke angesaugt und über
Kanäle zur Wärmerückgewinnung geführt. Die Wärmedämmverglasung liegt
dabei außen, während die zwischenliegenden transparenten Sonnenschutz-
Stoffstoren durch ein Einfachglas geschützt werden. Das TABS-System wird
mit drei Vorläufen [Hoch, Tief, Eckbüros] betrieben. Die nutzungsabhängigen
Vorlauftemperaturen werden in Abhängigkeit zur Wetterprognose für den Fol-
getag gesteuert. Die Kühlung erfolgt mit geringstem Energieaufwand vorwie-
gend während der Nachtstunden über die Außenluft. Dank des Selbstregulier-
effektes des TABS sind keine aufwändigen Zonen- und Raumregulierungen
notwendig. Für die Beleuchtung sorgen Ständerleuchten mit licht- und bewe-
gungsabhängiger Steuerung. Durch eine einfache und kostengünstige System-
technik können variable Wärmelasten bis 45 W/m² abgeführt werden und dies
weitgehend über freie Kühlung mit Außenluft [Adiabatische Rückkühler]. Die

e

Address
Hagenholzstrasse 20 / 22 / Andreasstrasse / Thurgauerstrasse 30 / 32 / 34 / 36 / 38,
CH-8050 Zurich

atelier ww Architekten SIA AG
Walter Wäschle, together with Urs Wüst, is co-owner of atelier ww, founded
in Zurich in 1970. Walter Wäschle graduated from the Academy of Fine Arts
in Vienna, Wüst from the Academy of Fine Arts in Düsseldorf.
The work of atelier ww comprises all areas of urban development and architecture. Many projects result from winning competitions. The portfolio encompasses a wide spectrum of buildings with a variety of uses and dimensions,
such as trade fair buildings, shopping centres, hotels, office and commercial
buildings, as well as industrial and residential buildings.

Client
BVK Personalvorsorge from the Canton of Zurich [»CS Towers« and »Vertex«].
BVK is the pension fund for employees of the Canton of Zurich, the largest
pension fund in Switzerland.
AXA Leben AG, represented by AXA Investment Managers Switzerland AG
[»Maintower«], Both companies are part of the AXA group, one of the world's
leading asset managers.

Building Structure / Key Data
The plot of land on Thurgauerstrasse has a surface area of 15.421 square
metres, of which the building occupies an area of 103,2 x 119,4 metres. The
ensemble consists of four buildings, grouped around a central interior square
called Quadroplatz: the double tower [CS] in the east, the southern high-
rise [Maintower/ AXA], the southern high-rise [Geschäftshaus/ BVK], and
the western smaller Stadthaus in between [Stadthaus/ BVK]. All four buildings
have a base with a height of 23,70 metres / seven floors, above which there
are four high-rise buildings with a height of 88 metres / 21 floors; 72,50 metres / 26 floors [CS]; 59,50 metres / 17 floors [AXA]; and 49,60 metres / 14
floors [BVK]. The standard floor height of the ensemble is 3,30 metres, on
the ground floor 3,80 metres. The buildings total 136,500 square metres of
floor area / 474,400 cubic metres of building volume, of which 60,000 square
metres of floor area / 215,000 cubic metres of building volume belong to the
CS building; 31,300 square metres of floor area / 16,740 cubic metres of
building volume belong to the AXA building; 31,300 square metres of floor
area / 106,800 cubic metres of building volume belong to the Geschäftshaus BVK; and 13,900 square metres of floor area / 45,950 cubic metres of
the building volume to the Stadthaus BVK.

Energy Concept
Through the intelligent integration of the façade, support structure, and technical features of the building, a modern and eco-friendly energy concept
was realized for all the buildings within the ensemble, which was certified
according to the Minergie standard. Three elements form the main features
of the space-saving, ecological, and economical energy concept: the ventilated façade, with sun protection in the space between the two layers; the
thermo active component systems for heating and cooling in the reinforced
concrete ceilings; and an efficient displacement ventilation system through
the double floors of the office areas. This ensures an optimal and pleasant
room climate, with moderate energy costs and low capital expenditure.
For the individual rooms, the air supply is processed centrally and distributed
to the rooms in a laminar flow via ground air vents. The exhaust air façade
draws the air up to the ceiling and into channels for heat recovery. The insulation glazing is external, whereas the transparent fabric awnings for sun
protection in between are protected by single glazing. The thermo active
building system [TABS] is operated in three flows [high, low, corner offices].
The usage-based flow temperatures are regulated according to the weather
forecast for the following day. Cooling takes place mostly at night, using
outdoor air with minimal energy consumption. Owing to the self-regulation
of the TABS, no complicated zone and room regulation is necessary. Lighting
is provided by standing lamps that are regulated by light and movement.
The simple and cost-effective system technology enables variable heat
loads of up to 45 W / square metre, mostly by means of free cooling with outdoor air [adiabatic heat exchangers]. The pleasant room temperatures –
under 26°C in summer – are particularly appreciated by the employees.

d

angenehmen Raumtemperaturen unter 26 °C im Sommer werden von den Mitarbeiterinnen und Mitarbeitern besonders geschätzt.

Der Wärmebezug erfolgt umweltschonend über das Fernwärmeversorgungsnetz der Stadt Zürich, welches aus der Kehrichtverbrennungsanlage Hagenholz gespeist wird. Nach der hydraulischen Trennung werden die Heizgruppen – Lufterhitzer und statische Heizung – gleitend bis max. 45° C Vorlauf versorgt. Das Brauchwarmwasser für die Officeküchen der Büros wird dezentral über Wärmepumpenboiler elektrisch erzeugt, um Zirkulationsverluste komplett zu eliminieren. Dabei wird die Abwärme der Elektroverteilräume genutzt. In jedem Haus sind jeweils hocheffiziente Turbocorkältemaschinen für die primäre Kälteproduktion zuständig. Aus Gründen der Redundanz und für die Mieterausbauten werden zusätzlich Kältemaschinen mit Schraubenverdichtern eingesetzt. Die verwendeten Kältemittel ermöglichen sogar den Einsatz einer Wärmerückgewinnung zu Heizzwecken, bei dem die Abwärme wieder in das Heizsystem eingespeist wird. Insbesondere in den Wintermonaten wird somit die Abwärme der technischen Ausrüstungen [Serverräume usw. ...] optimal zurückgewonnen. Die überschüssige Abwärme der Kältemaschinen wird über Hybridkühler über Dach vernichtet. Durch Verdunstungskühlung werden tiefstmögliche Rückkühltemperaturen für einen hocheffizienten Kälteprozess möglich.

Erschließung

Die Haupterschließungen aller vier Gebäude des Ensembles erfolgen für die Fußgänger über den Quadro-Platz im Zentrum, im Fall des Stadthauses von den auf den Platz führenden Gassen. Die Eingangsfoyers, welche den Liftfoyers der einzelnen Häuser zugeordnet sind, werden über die dem Platz zugeordneten Kolonnaden erschlossen. Der Doppelturm [CS] besitzt ein durchgestecktes Foyer, das sowohl vom Platz als auch von dem östlichen Vorplatz zugänglich ist. Der Doppelturm besitzt ein weiteres Foyer zum Platz, welches eine getrennte Erschließung beider Türme ermöglicht. Auf dem östlichen Vorplatz [Marie-Curie-Platz] befinden sich die Rampen für die Erschließung mit Personenwagen und Lastwagen. Über diese Rampe erfolgt die Anlieferung und Entsorgung für alle Häuser im zweiten Untergeschoss des Ensembles. Zusätzlich stehen oberirdische Vorfahrten zu den einzelnen Gebäuden mit Besucherparkplätzen und Veloabstellplätzen zur Verfügung. Die vertikale Erschließung erfolgt von den Eingangsfoyers jeweils hausweise über Lifte und Treppenhäuser.

Fassade

Die Fassade erfüllt hohe Anforderungen an Wärmeschutz, Sonnenschutz, Entrauchung und Sicherheit und ist außerdem Teil der Raumbelüftung. Sie ist als Vorhangfassade aus Glas und Naturstein ausgebildet. Technisch gesehen handelt es sich um eine zweischalige Abluftfassade, die mit der Lüftungsanlage kombiniert ist.

Die Fassadenelemente aus isolierten Leichtmetallprofilen sind in zwei Typen raumhoher Felder unterteilt: ein transparentes und ein nichttransparentes. Beim transparenten Feld sind außenseitig ein Rauchabzugsflügel mit einer Wärmeschutzverglasung und raumseitig ein verglaster Drehflügel eingesetzt. Der bewegliche Sonnenschutz mit Vertikalmarkisen aus halbtransparenten, silbrig reflektierenden Storen ist im belüfteten Zwischenraum angeordnet und mit einer automatischen Steuerung ausgerüstet. Die Belüftung des Fassadenzwischenraumes wird durch einen mechanischen Luftabzug im Hohlboden sichergestellt, wobei die verbrauchte Raumluft im Sturzbereich in das Fassadenelement eingeleitet wird. Das nichttransparente Feld der Fassade ist mit einer Sandwichfüllung belegt. Außenseitig ist ein geschliffener Naturstein [Cape Green Syenit aus Bitter Fontein, Südafrika] flächenbündig mit der äußeren Wärmeschutzverglasung auf das Fassadenelement montiert. Raumseitig ist das Sandwich mit einer gipsgebundenen Spanplatte verkleidet. Die Konstruktion erlaubt eine freie Wahl des Produktions- und Montageablaufs. Die einzelnen Fassadenelemente können sowohl als fertige Elemente [inkl. eingebautem Sonnenschutz und innerem Flügel] geliefert und versetzt oder in mehreren Schritten montiert werden. Im Attikageschoss sind die Fenster gegenüber der Natursteinfassade um 20 Zentimeter zurückversetzt. In diesem Bereich sind bei allen Gebäuden Nistkästen für Mauersegler im Hohlraum hinter dem Naturstein eingebaut. Das Anflugloch befindet sich auf der wetterabgewandten Seite im Laibungsstein. Die äußere Gebäudereinigung erfolgt mit Fassadenbefahranlagen. Die festinstallierten Anlagen mit Schienensystem und Laufwagen mit Kranausleger sind auf den Flachdächern platziert. Die Anlagen sind mit zusätzlichen Seilwinden ausgerüstet, die das Aufziehen von einzelnen Glaselementen erlauben. Dadurch ist jederzeit ein Glasersatz von außen gewährleistet.

e

The eco-friendly heating is supplied by the district heating supply network of the city of Zurich, which is powered by the Hagenholz waste incinerator. After the hydraulic separation, the heating circuits – air heaters and static heating – are supplied with a continuous flow of a maximum of 45°C. The hot water supply for the office kitchens is generated electrically by decentralized heat pump boilers, to eliminate circulation losses completely. The waste heat from the electrical distribution room is used in the process. In each building, the primary cooling is produced by highly efficient Turbocor refrigerating machines. For redundancy reasons and for tenant expansions, additional cooling machines with screw compressors are used. These cooling methods even enable the integration of heat recovery for heating purposes, by feeding the waste heat back into the heating system. Especially in the winter months, this ensures the optimal recovery of waste heat from the technical facilities [server rooms, etc.]. The excess waste heat from the cooling machines is destroyed by hybrid coolers over the roof. Evaporative cooling enables the lowest possible recooling temperatures for a highly efficient cooling process.

Access

For pedestrians, the main access points of all four buildings in the ensemble are via the Quadroplatz square in the centre, and in the case of the Stadthaus, from the alleys leading to the square. The entrance foyers and the adjoining lift foyers of each building are accessed via the colonnades on the square. The double tower [CS] has a through foyer that it accessible both from the square and from the eastern forecourt. The double tower has a further foyer facing the square, which enables separate access to each tower. On the eastern forecourt [Marie-Curie-Platz] there are ramps for car and van access. These ramps are also used for deliveries and waste disposal for all the units, on the second basement level. In addition, there are ground-level access driveways up to each of the buildings, with visitor parking spaces and bicycle stands. Vertical access is provided by lifts and stairwells from the entrance foyers of each building.

Façade

The façade meets high standards in terms of insulation, sun protection, smoke extraction, and safety, and is also part of the room ventilation. It is conceived as a curtain wall made of glass and natural stone. From a technical point of view, it is a double-layered exhaust air façade, which is combined with a ventilation system.

The façade elements, consisting of insulated light metal profiles, are divided into two types of floor-to-ceiling sections: one is transparent and the other one is non-transparent. The transparent section incorporates an external flue with insulated glazing, and internally a glazed rotor. Flexible sun protection is provided by vertical awnings of semi-transparent, silvery, reflecting fabric, mounted in the ventilated interspace and fitted with automatic controls. The ventilation of the façade interspace is ensured by a mechanical air exhaust in the hollow floor, whereby the used indoor air is drawn into the façade element in the lintel area. The non-transparent section of the façade is sandwiched between two layers. Externally, polished natural stone [Cape Green Synite from Bitter Fontein, South Africa] is mounted onto the façade element, flush with the external insulation glazing. On the inner side, it is clad with gypsum-bonded chipboard. The structure allows a free choice of production and mounting procedures. The individual façade elements can either be delivered and processed as ready-made elements [including built-in sun protection and inner wing], or assembled in several steps. On the attic floor, the windows are recessed twenty centimetres from the natural stone façade. In this area, all buildings have nesting boxes for swifts built into the hollow cavity behind the natural stone. The entrance hole is in the soffit stone on the side sheltered from the weather. The exterior of the building can be cleaned by means of mobile façade maintenance units. The permanently installed units, with a rail system and carriages with crane jibs, are positioned on the flat roofs. The units are fitted with additional cable winches, which enable individual glass elements to be lifted up. This allows the glass to be replaced from the outside at any time.

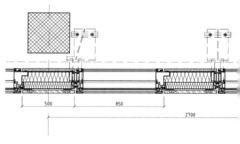

Elementierte Fassade: Detailgrundriss
Segmented façade: detailed layout

Fassade aus geschliffenem Granit
[Cape Green Syenit aus Bitter Fontein, Südafrika]
Façade made of smoothed granite
[Cape Green Syenit from Bitter Fontein, South Africa]

d

Fotografie

Olivia Heussler wurde 1957 in Zürich geboren. Ihre Anfänge als Fotografin liegen im Fotojournalismus. Heute arbeitet sie überwiegend an Langzeitprojekten, die sie medienübergreifend präsentiert. Ihre Bilder, Filme und Projektionen sind in zahlreichen Museums- und Galerieausstellungen in Deutschland, der Schweiz sowie in London, Paris, New York, Jerusalem und Managua zu sehen. Olivia Heussler ist in renommierten Sammlungen wie der Fotostiftung Schweiz in Winterthur, dem Musée de l'Elysée in Lausanne oder der Bibliothèque Nationale in Paris vertreten. Viele ihrer Projekte sind auch in Buchform publiziert. Zuletzt sind erschienen Zürich, »Sommer 1980« [2010] und »El sueño de Solentiname« [IHNCA-UCA 2010].

Stefan Müller wurde 1965 in Bonn geboren. Er studierte Visuelle Kommunikation an der Fachhochschule in Dortmund. Er wurde von O. M. Ungers als Architekturfotograf entdeckt und fotografierte ab 1992 seine Bauten. Seit 1994 arbeitet er von Berlin aus unter anderem für die Architekten Max Dudler, Kleihues + Kleihues, Ortner & Ortner, Barkow Leibinger und Müller Reimann.

Planungsgeschichte

Das ehemalige Areal der Kugellagerfabrik FAG wurde zuletzt durch den Autoimporteur AMAG als Standplatz für einen Gebrauchtwagenhandel genutzt. Implenia bzw. ihre Vorgängerfirma Göhner-Merkur hatte das Projekt entwickelt und das atelier ww mit den ersten Überbauungskonzepten bzw. Projektstudien für das Grundstück beauftragt. Die dabei entstandene Idee einer Hochhausüberbauung – die erste in Zürich nach 20 Jahren – war Anstoß zu den städtischen Kooperativen Entwicklungsplanungen »Quartier Leutschenbach« [1998] und der »Zusatzstudie Bahnhof Oerlikon-Ost« [2000], die, neben anderen Erkenntnissen, das Areal als Hochhausstandort bestätigten. Zur Steuerung des Vorhabens wurde von Seiten der Stadt Zürich ein neuartiges Instrument geschaffen: das Baukollegium bestehend aus anerkannten Architekten, Städtebauern und Vertretern der Stadt. 1999 bestätigte das Baukollegium den Standort für die Hochhausüberbauung. Die Stadt Zürich als genehmigende Behörde verlangte, dass für den Fall einer Hochhausbebauung ein Architekt mit internationaler Erfahrung in der Planung von Hochhäusern herbeizuziehen sei. Das atelier ww bildete daraufhin eine Arbeitsgemeinschaft mit Max Dudler. Im Frühjahr 2000 genehmigte die Bausektion des Stadtrates von Zürich den Bau des Doppelturmes [CS], dessen Bauarbeiten von April 2000 bis Ende 2004 andauerten. Im März 2001 konnte die Arbeitsgemeinschaft atelier ww / Max Dudler auch den internationalen Projektwettbewerb für die Bebauung des westlichen Teils für sich entscheiden. Die Überarbeitung ihres Projektes »Stadtfigur« wurde im Juli 2002 vom Preisgericht bestätigt und bildete die Grundlage für einen privaten Gestaltungsplan für das Grundstück. Die Bauarbeiten zum zweiten und dritten Bauabschnitt, welche die Ensemblewirkung des Gesamtprojektes erst wirksam werden ließen, wurden im Jahr 2010 aufgenommen und Ende 2013 fertiggestellt. Implenia zeichnete als Totalunternehmerin für die Realisierung des Gesamtprojekts verantwortlich.

Gebäudestruktur / Flexibilität

Die Nutzflächen des Hochhausensembles wurden nicht auf eine bestimmte Nutzung / einen bestimmten Nutzer zugeschnitten. Aus diesem Grund wurden Flexibilität und Modularität zu den bestimmenden Prinzipien der Grundrissorganisation. Alle vier Häuser sind mit innenliegenden Erschließungskernen disponiert. Der Kern fasst sämtliche fixen Neben-, Verkehrs- und Funktionsflächen. Zwischen seinen tragenden Wänden und den vor der Fassadenebene stehenden Stützen spannen die stützenfrei weitgehend frei bespielbare Nutzflächen. Im Sinne einer größtmöglichen Variabilität sind alle Installationen [Heizung, Lüftung, Sanitär, Beleuchtung, Energieversorgung, EDV-Medien] in einem Ausbauraster in beiden Richtungen so geplant, dass möglichst viele Teilungs- und Nutzungsvarianten offen bleiben. Die Erschließung [und Größe] der Büros sowie der dazugehörenden öffentlichen und halböffentlichen Flächen ist so geplant, dass durch deren Anordnung ebenfalls eine hohe Flexibilität gewährleistet ist. Die Fassadengestaltung verschleiert diese Neutralität in Bezug auf die Nutzung nicht. Die Allgemeingültigkeit der Architektur wird sogar Thema der Fassadengestaltung. Die starke Identität des Ensembles beruht auf dieser Umwertung.

Planungsteam

Architekten: Arbeitsgemeinschaft atelier ww Architekten SIA AG und Max Dudler Architekten AG
Landschaftsarchitektur: Planetage GmbH, Zürich

e

Photography

Olivia Heussler was born in 1957 in Zurich. Her photographic career began with photojournalism. Today she works primarily on long-term projects, which she presents in different media. Her pictures, films, and projections can be seen in numerous museum and gallery exhibitions in Germany, Switzerland, London, Paris, New York, Jerusalem, and Managua. Olivia Heussler is represented in renowned collections, such as the Fotostiftung Schweiz in Winterthur, the Musée de l'Elysée in Lausanne, or the Bibliothèque Nationale in Paris. Many of her projects have also been published in book form. Recent publications are Zürich, »Sommer 1980« [2010] and »El sueño de Solentiname« [IHNCA-UCA 2010].

Stefan Müller was born in 1965 in Bonn. He studied Visual Communication at the Technical University in Dortmund. He was discovered as an architectural photographer by O. M. Ungers, whose buildings he has photographed since 1992. Since 1994, he has been based in Berlin, working for the architects Max Dudler, Kleihues + Kleihues, Ortner & Ortner, Barkow Leibinger, and Müller Reimann, amongst others.

Planning History

The former site of the FAG ball bearing factory was used most recently by the car importer AMAG as a location for a used car dealership. Implenia and its predecessor company, Göhner-Merkur, had developed the project and appointed atelier ww to draw up the first development concepts and project studies for the site. The resulting idea of a high-rise development – the first in Zurich for twenty years – was the impetus for the municipal cooperative development plans for Quartier Leutschenbach [1998] and the supplementary study Oerlikon-Ost railway station [2000], which alongside other conclusions confirmed the site as a location for high-rises. In order to manage the project, the Zurich municipal authorities created an innovative tool: a construction committee consisting of renowned architects, urban planners, and municipal representatives. In 1999, the construction committee confirmed the site for the high-rise development. The city of Zurich, as the approving authority, required that in the case of a high-rise development, an architect with international experience in the planning of high-rises had to be consulted. Consequently, atelier ww entered into a working cooperation with Max Dudler. In spring 2000, the building department of the Zurich city council approved the construction of the double tower [CS], with building work lasting from April 2000 to the end of 2004. In March 2001, the cooperation of atelier ww / Max Dudler also won the international project competition for the building of the western section. The reworking of their »Stadtfigur« [Urban Emblem] project was confirmed by the jury in July 2002 and formed the basis for a private design plan for the site. The construction work for the second and third building sections, which enabled the realization of the overall ensemble, was started in 2010 and completed at the end of 2013. Implenia was responsible for the realization of the overall project as general contractor.

Building Structure / Flexibility

The floor spaces of the high-rise ensemble were not customized for particular uses or specific users. Flexibility and modularity were the guiding principles of the layout arrangement. All four buildings have interior access cores. The core comprises a number of specified secondary, infrastructural, and functional areas. Unsupported areas stretch between its supporting walls and the columns standing in front of the façade, which are to a large extent open to free usage. In the interests of the greatest possible variability, all of the installations – heating, ventilation, sanitary, lighting, energy supply, EDP media – are planned in a structural grid in both directions, in such a way that they enable as many configurations and usages as possible. The accesses to the offices, their size, as well as the associated public and semi-public areas, are planned so that their layout also ensures a high degree of flexibility. The façade design does not disguise this usage neutrality. The generality of the architecture is even reflected in the façade design. The strong identity of the ensemble is based on this coherence.

Planning Team

Architects: cooperation between atelier ww Architekten SIA AG and Max Dudler Architekten AG
Landscape architecture: Planetage GmbH, Zurich

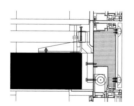

Fassadenschnitt und Detail
Façade cross section and detail

d

Statik: Arbeitsgemeinschaft Henauer Gugler AG, Zürich und Eichenberger AG, Zürich
Gebäudetechnik: Arbeitsgemeinschaft Gruenberg & Partner AG, Zürich / Reuss Engineering AG, Gisikon / Schneider Engineering & Partner, Zürich
MSRL: Reuss Engineering, Winterthur und Sigren Engieering AG, Glattbrugg
Bauphysik: Leuthardt & Mäder, Brüttisellen
Brandschutzplaner: Hautle Anderegg & Partner AG, Bern
Fassadenplaner: Stäger & Nägeli AG, Zürich
Lichtplaner: Mettler + Partner Licht AG, Zürich

Realisation / Totalunternehmer
Implenia Schweiz AG, Dietikon

Investition
Die Gesamtinvestition beläuft sich auf 423 Millionen CHF, davon entfallen 210 Millionen CHF auf den Doppelturm [CS], 100 Millionen CHF auf den Bauteil »Maintower« [AXA] und 113 Millionen CHF auf Geschäftshaus und Stadthaus [BVK].

Lichtgestaltung
Bei der Entwicklung der Lichtlösung für den Außenraum der Hochhausüberbauung Quadro wurde das Hauptaugenmerk auf die Zugänge und den inneren Platz gelegt. Die Lichtgestaltung soll eine polyvalente Benutzbarkeit sicherstellen und zugleich auch in den Abend- und Nachtstunden die Geschwisterhäuser als Ensemble spürbar machen. Vier Durchgänge führen zwischen den einzelnen Gebäuden zum inneren Stadtraum, der dreiseitig durch Arkaden gefasst wird. Durch fassadennahe Lichtbänder werden die Arkadengänge gleichmäßig und großzügig ausgeleuchtet. Das mittlere Feld des urbanen Platzraums ist leicht abgesenkt. Massive Poller aus Naturstein begrenzen und definieren diese innere Fläche. In die Poller integrierte LED-Strahler markieren das aufgezogene Feld. Dadurch entsteht eine Differenzierung der öffentlichen Bewegungsflächen. Durch speziell gerichtete Lamellen, die seitlich flächenbündig in den Poller eingelassen wurden, trifft das Licht blendfrei auf die Bodenfläche. Richtstrahler, die auf Masten oder in architektonische Elemente integriert werden konnten, geben den Zugängen zwischen den Gebäuden zum inneren Platz hin sowie den Fahrradständern einen sanften Lichtteppich.

Max Dudler
Max Dudler wurde in Altenrhein in der Schweiz geboren, er studierte Architektur an der Frankfurter Städelschule und an der Hochschule der Künste Berlin. Zu Beginn seiner Laufbahn arbeitete er bei Oswald Mathias Ungers. 1992 gründete er ein eigenes Architekturbüro. Heute betreibt das Büro Niederlassungen in Berlin, Zürich und Frankfurt. Seit 2004 unterrichtet Max Dudler an der Kunstakademie Düsseldorf.

Materialien
Die Architektur des Ensembles ist auf wenige Formen, Elemente und Materialien reduziert. Alle Fassaden bestehen aus Glas, eingefasst in pulverbeschichtete Aluminiumrahmen und Granit. Es handelt sich um einen Cape Green Synit aus Bitter Fontein, Südafrika, der in verschiedenen Oberflächenausführungen verwendet wird. Der Granit wurde auch für Teile der horizontalen Flächen sowie in den Foyerbereichen verwendet.

Nutzer und Namen
Hauptmieterin und -nutzerin des Doppelturms [CS] ist die Credit Suisse Group AG. Credit Suisse belegt auch einen Teil des südlichen Geschäftshauses [BVK]. Im Erdgeschoss dieses Gebäudeteils ist ein Medgate Health Center untergebracht. Der »Maintower« im Norden wird von der Versicherung AXA Winterthur und dem Unternehmen Novo Nordisk genutzt. Im Erdgeschoss befindet sich neben kleineren Retaileinheiten ein Coop-Pronto-Supermarkt. Die derzeitigen und ehemaligen Mieter und Vermarkter haben die Namen geprägt, unter denen das Hochhausensemble Thurgauerstrasse in der Öffentlichkeit bekannt ist. Der Doppelturm, der heute unter dem Namen CS-Towers bekannt ist, lief früher unter der Bezeichnung diAx-Tower, später unter Sunrise Tower. Das Gesamtensemble wurde unter dem Namen »Quadro« vermarktet, wobei der nordöstliche Teil als »Maintower« und der südwestliche mit dem Geschäftshaus und dem Stadthaus als »Vertex« vermietet wurde.

e

Structural engineering: cooperation between Henauer Gugler, Zürich and Eichenberger AG, Zürich
Building services engineering: cooperation between Gruenberg & Partner AG, Zurich / Reuss Engineering AG, Gisikon / Schneider Engineering & Partner, Zurich
Building automation: Reuss Engineering, Winterthur and Sigren Engineering AG, Glattbrugg
Structural physics: Leuthardt & Mäder, Brüttisellen
Fire safety planners: Hautle Anderegg & Partner AG, Bern
Façade planners: Stäger & Nägeli AG, Zurich
Lighting designers: Mettler + Partner Licht AG, Zurich

Realisation / General Contractor
Implenia Schweiz AG, Dietikon

Investment
The total investment amounts to 423 million CHF, of which 210 million CHF are allocated to the double tower [CS], 100 million CHF to the »Maintower« building [AXA], and 113 million CHF to Geschäftshaus and Stadthaus [BVK].

Lighting Design
During the development of the lighting solution for the outdoor spaces of the Quadro high-rise development, the main focus was on the entrances and the inner square. The lighting was designed to ensure polyvalent usage and to make the surrounding buildings perceptible as an ensemble in the evening and at night. Four passageways lead between the individual buildings to the inner urban space, which is surrounded on three sides by arcades that are illuminated evenly and generously by means of strips of light near the façade. The middle section of the urban square is slightly lowered. Solid natural stone bollards delimit and define this inner area. LED spots integrated into the bollards mark the raised area around it. This differentiates the public areas of movement. Through specially oriented lamella, flush-mounted on the sides of the bollards, the light shines glare-free on the ground. Directional beams, which were integrated on masts or into architectural elements, provide a soft carpet of light for the passageways between the buildings to the inner square, as well as for the bicycle stands.

Max Dudler
Max Dudler was born in Altenrhein in Switzerland. He studied architecture at the Frankfurter Städelschule and at the Hochschule der Künste Berlin [University of the Arts]. At the beginning of his career he worked for Oswald Mathias Ungers. In 1992, he founded his own architecture office. Today it has branches in Berlin, Zurich, and Frankfurt. Since 2004, Max Dudler has been teaching at the Kunstakademie Düsseldorf [Art Academy].

Materials
The architecture of the ensemble is reduced to few forms, elements, and materials. All the façades consist of glass, set into powder-coated aluminium frames and granite. Cape Green Synite from Bitter Fontein, South Africa is used in different surface applications. The granite was also used for parts of the horizontal surfaces, as well as in the foyer areas.

Users and Names
The main tenant and user of the double tower [CS] is the Credit Suisse Group AG. Credit Suisse also occupies part of the southern Geschäftshaus [BVK]. Medgate Health Center is on the ground floor of this section of the building. The »Maintower« in the north is used by the insurance company AXA Winterthur and the company Novo Nordisk. On the ground floor, there are smaller retail units and a Coop Pronto supermarket. The current and former tenants and marketers have determined the names by which the high-rise ensemble on Thurgauerstrasse is known to the public. The double tower, which is now known as CS Towers, used to be called diAx Tower, later Sunrise Tower. The whole ensemble was marketed under the name »Quadro«, whereby the north-eastern part was let as »Maintower« and the south-western part – with the Geschäftshaus and the Stadthaus – as »Vertex«.

Das Leutschenbachquartier mit Blick Richtung Norden um 1963
The Leutschenbach district with a view to the north around 1963

Max Dudler

d

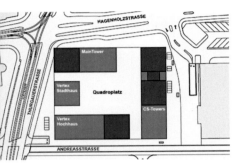

Lageplan mit Hausbezeichnungen
Site plan with labeled buildings

Bürolandschaft eines Regelgeschosses
Office landscape of a standard floor

Flur
Hallway

Planungsteam Architektur
Architektur: Max Dudler [MD]
Gesamtleitung: Danilo Morellini, atelier ww [aww]: operativ, Christian Moeller Deplazes, Max Dudler [MD]
Projektleitung: Konrad Mäder Labhard [aww], Bauteil AXA und BVK, Andreas Brunner [aww], Bauteil AXA
Ausführung: Valentin Niessen [MD], Daniel Noser [aww]
Wettbewerb: Britta Fritze [MD], Simeon Heinzl [MD], Bernhard Moeller [MD], Christian Moeller Deplazes [MD], Danilo Morellini [aww], Phil Peterson [MD]
Team Planung: Carolin Balkenhol [MD], Barbara Dafft [MD], Britta Fritze [MD], Francesca Guido [aww], Pascal Gmür [aww], Aysu Gümüstekin [MD], Clive Hildering [MD], Judith Hobi [aww], Javier Horrach [aww], Andreas Kobelt [aww], Thomas Künzle [MD], Tina Mustapic [aww], Eva Pigulla [aww], Kwangmann Park [aww], René Salzmann [MD], Tobias Schaer [MD], Simone Schefer [aww], Annette Schmitt [aww], Georg Schönborn [MD], Christoph Stäubli [aww]

Platzgestaltung / Außenraum
Die Türme des Hochhausensembles umschließen einen klar definierten Binnenplatz, der durch publikumsorientierte Nutzungen in den Erdgeschossen belebt wird. Der Platz soll im Winter wie im Sommer durch öffentliche Veranstaltungen und Freiraumaktivitäten genutzt werden. Die horizontale Fläche ergänzt als »fünfte Fassade« aus dunkelgrünem Natursteinbelag die umliegenden Fassaden gleichen Materials zu einer Gesamtfigur. In der Platzmitte ist eine leichte Vertiefung, in der einzelne Wasserflächen definiert sind.
Die Freiflächengestaltung der Umräume der urbanen Stadtinsel soll die jeweils vorhandenen unterschiedlichen Charaktermerkmale herausarbeiten. Entlang der Thurgauerstrasse begrenzt eine Platanenreihe das Areal. Die großzügige Fläche zwischen Straße und Fassaden ist als Ankunfts- und Verteilungsort für Fußgänger, die vom Bahnhof Oerlikon oder von der Station der Stadtbahn kommen, gestaltet. Asphalt- und Kiesflachen rhythmisieren und gliedern diese Vorzone.
Die übergeordnete Fußgänger- und Fahrradverbindung Andreasstrasse entlang des Bahndamms ist als wichtige Orientierungsachse linear strukturiert. Hier bildet dichte Vegetation einen Kontrast zu dem von Hartflächen und Großbauten dominierten Quartier. Eine lange Sitzbank am Hangfuß definiert das Ufer des Bachs. Nachts wird die Vegetation mit Hilfe von Licht zur tiefgrünen Kulisse. Vor den Fassaden stehen geschnittene Baumkörper in bepflanzten Flächen, welche Velorampe, Abluftkamine, Not-Treppenaufgänge der Tiefgarage und Rauchgasöffnungen zu einem raumbildenden Element zusammenfassen. Der Marie-Curie-Platz zwischen dem Doppelturm und Parkhaus Messe ist als offene Fläche asphaltiert Eine parallel zur Fassade verlaufende Reihe hoher Beleuchtungskandelaber markiert die Verbindung zwischen Messe und Hagenholzstrasse. An der von einer Baumreihe begleiteten Hagenholzstrasse wird der breite Trottoirraum zur Erschließung des Areals durch eine Vorfahrt mit Besucherparkplätzen genutzt. Die hier angeordneten Nottreppenaufgänge und Abluftkamine sind durch ihre Detaillierung in die Außenraumgestaltung integriert.

Parkingkonzept
Die Tiefgaragenanlage für Personenwagen im ersten und zweiten Tiefgeschoss bietet insgesamt 501 Plätze. 279 Plätze sind für den Doppelturm [CS], 99 Plätze für das Geschäftshaus [BVK], 9 für das Stadthaus [BVK] und 79 Plätze für den Maintower [AXA] reserviert.

Raumprogramm
Das Hochhausensemble Thurgauerstrasse stellt auf 73.704 Quadratmeter Nutzfläche Raum für 4.700 Arbeitsplätze bereit. Die Erdgeschosszonen sind für öffentliche Funktionen wie Erschließungsfoyers und öffentliche Nutzungen wie Cafés, Restaurants und Geschäfte eingerichtet. Etabliert haben sich bereits ein Café, ein Restaurant, ein großes Mitarbeiterrestaurant, ein großer Konferenzbereich, ein Supermarkt, ein Florist, ein Sandwichladen, ein medizinisches Versorgungszentrum sowie ein Fitnesscenter im Turm des Geschäftshauses Süd.

Städtebauliche Situation
Das Hochhausensemble liegt im Stadtteil Leutschenbach in Zürich-Nord an der Einfallsachse vom Flughafen Kloten zur City. In dem schnell gewachsenen Quartier treffen städtische und vorstädtische Elemente unvermittelt aufeinander:

e

Architectural Planning Team
Overall management: Danilo Morellini, atelier ww [aww]: operations, Christian Moeller Deplazes, Max Dudler [MD]: architecture
Project management: Konrad Mäder Labhard [aww], AXA and BVK buildings, Andreas Brunner [aww], AXA building
Realization: Valentin Niessen [MD], Daniel Noser [aww]
Competition: Britta Fritze [MD], Simeon Heinzl [MD], Bernhard Moeller [MD], Christian Moeller Deplazes [MD], Danilo Morellini [aww], Phil Peterson [MD]
Team planning: Carolin Balkenhol [MD], Barbara Dafft [MD], Britta Fritze [MD],Francesca Guido [aww], Pascal Gmür [aww], Aysu Gümüstekin [MD], Clive Hildering [MD], Judith Hobi [aww], Javier Horrach [aww], Andreas Kobelt [aww], Thomas Künzle [MD], Tina Mustapic [aww], Eva Pigulla [aww], Kwangmann Park [aww], René Salzmann [MD], Tobias Schaer [MD], Simone Schefer [aww], Annette Schmitt [aww], Georg Schönborn [MD], Christoph Stäubli [aww]

Square Design / Outdoor Area
The towers of the high-rise ensemble surround a clearly defined interior square, which is enlivened by publicly oriented usages on the ground floor. The square is to be used both in winter and in summer for public events and outdoor activities. The horizontal surface, as the »fifth façade« with a dark green natural stone surface, complements the surrounding façades of the same material, forming a coherent whole. In the middle of the square, there is a slightly lowered area, containing individual water features.
The design of the open spaces around the urban island is intended to emphasize the various respective characteristics. Along Thurgauerstrasse, a row of plane trees borders the site. The spacious area between the street and the façades is designed as an arrival and transit area for pedestrians coming from Oerlikon train station or from the tram stop. Asphalted and pebbled surfaces rhythmize and structure this entrance area.
As an important orientation axis, Andreasstrasse – the major pedestrian and cycle thoroughfare along the rail embankment – has a linear structure. Here, dense vegetation forms a contrast to the district dominated by hard surfaces and large buildings. A long seating bench at the foot of the slope defines the bank of the stream. At night, lighting turns the vegetation into a deep green backdrop. Chopped tree trunks stand in front of the façades, in planted areas that form a structuring spatial element, bringing together cycle ramps, exhaust chimneys, emergency exit staircases from the underground garage, and flue gas vents. The Marie-Curie-Platz between the double tower and the trade fair parking block is asphalted as an open space. A row of high street lamps running parallel to the façade marks the link between the trade fair and Hagenholzstrasse. The wide sidewalk area along Hagenholzstrasse, lined with a row of trees, is used as access to the site, with an access driveway that has visitor parking spaces. The emergency exit stairwells and exhaust chimneys here are integrated into the design of the outdoor space through their detail.

Parking Concept
The underground garage for cars, on the first and second basement levels, provides a total of 501 spaces, of which 279 spaces are reserved for the double tower [CS], 99 spaces for the Geschäftshaus [BVK], 9 for the Stadthaus [BVK] and 79 spaces for the Maintower [AXA].

Spatial Programme
The high-rise ensemble on Thurgauerstrasse provides room for 4,700 workspaces across a usable floor space of 73,704 metres. The ground-floor zones are set up for public functions, such as access foyers and public usages, including cafés, restaurants, and shops. A café, a restaurant, a large staff restaurant, a large conference area, a supermarket, a florist, a sandwich shop, a medical, and a fitness centre have already been established in the tower of the southern Geschäftshaus.

Urban Development Situation
The high-rise ensemble is located in the Leutschenbach district in Zurich-Nord, on the axis that runs from Kloten Airport to the city. The district has grown rapidly and is characterized by a juxtaposition of urban and suburban elements: the rail embankment covered with dense vegetation borders the

d

Der von dichter Vegetation bewachsene Bahndamm grenzt an die großmaßstäblichen Hallen der Messe Zürich, welche von Autohändlern und kleinteiligen Siedlungshäusern umgeben ist. Entlang der sogenannten Glattalbahn, die dem Verlauf der Thurgauer Strasse folgt, sind darüber hinaus Dienstleistungscluster entstanden. Der private Gestaltungsplan für das Areal weist eine zulässige Ausnützungsziffer von 420 Prozent aus.

Tragwerk

Die Gebäude wurden mittels verrohrter Bohrpfähle auf einer Molassefelsschicht abgestellt, die auf dem Grundstück in 18 bis 28 Meter Tiefe unter künstlichen Auffüllungen, Seeablagerungen und Moräne vorgefunden wurde. In den Bereichen, in denen die Untergeschosse nicht überbaut wurden [Platz], dienen sie als Zugpfähle gegen Auftrieb. Dies war erforderlich, da Grundwasserspiegelmessungen zeigten, dass der obere freie Grundwasserspiegel nur ca. 1,2 Meter unter Terrain liegt.

In etwa 14 Metern Tiefe wird das Grundstück diagonal durch die Linienführung des Abwassertunnels Glatt-Stollen gekreuzt. Es handelt sich um ein Rohr von gut fünf Metern Durchmesser, welches nicht tangiert werden durfte. Die Pfähle durften erst in einem Abstand von fünf Metern von der Stollenachse gebohrt werden. Für die Abfangung der Stützenlasten über den Glatt-Stollen war eine 1,4 bis 1,8 Meter dicke, vorgespannte Bodenplatte notwendig. Die Bodenplatte musste in Etappen von drei Metern Breite erstellt werden, damit über dem Glatt-Stollen genügend Gewicht gegen den Auftrieb vorhanden war.

Um eine möglichst große Nutzungsflexibilität zu erreichen, wurde der Rohbau der vier Türme und der Sockelbauten als Skelettbau mit einem großzügigen Stützenraster ausgeführt. Die Decken sind vom Kern bis zur Fassade frei gespannt und haben eine Stärke von 26 bis 28 Zentimetern. Sie wurden als teilweise vorgespannte Ortbetondecken ausgeführt, da nur so die folgenden anspruchsvollen Anforderungen erreicht werden konnten: Geringe Konstruktionshöhe [beim 90-Meter-Turm konnte dadurch ein zusätzliches Geschoss realisiert werden], Reduktion des Eigengewichts, Brandschutz und Realisierbarkeit des thermoaktiven Bauteilsystems.

Die Erdbebenbemessung wurde mit dem Antwortspektrenverfahren durchgeführt. Bei diesem werden in einer dynamischen Berechnung neben der Grundschwingungsform auch die maßgebend angeregten höheren Eigenschwingungsformen berücksichtigt. Dabei den Türmen von 90 und 70 Metern in einer Richtung der Kern zur Turmhöhe betrachtet sehr schmal ist, wurden im 17. und 18. Obergeschoss zur Stabilisierung je zwei Betonwände erstellt, die vom Kern bis zu den Fassadenstützen reichen. Die Kernwände sind 40 Zentimeter stark und mit einem Beton B 45/35 erstellt worden. Die maximale Auslenkung des 88-Meter-Turms infolge von Wind beträgt gemäß Berechnung 44 Millimeter.

Velostation

Die 141 Veloabstellplätze in der Tiefgarage sind über eine Velorampe am Bahndamm an der Andreasstrasse zugänglich. Dieser Teil der Garage hat eigene Fluchttreppenhäuser.

Zürich-Nord

Leutschenbach ist eines der großen Entwicklungsgebiete der Stadt Zürich. Das ehemalige Industriegebiet in Zürich-Nord umfasst eine Fläche von rund 60 Hektar. Unter dem Eindruck der ersten Projektstudien zum Hochhausensemble startete die Stadt 1998 gemeinsam mit den privaten GrundeigentümerInnen eine kooperative Entwicklungsplanung für Leutschenbach. Das dabei entstandene Entwicklungsleitbild war Grundlage der aktuellen Bau- und Zonenordnung. Aufgrund seiner Lage hat sich Zürich-Nord zu einem strategisch relevanten Stadtteil innerhalb des Schweizer Finanz- und Wirtschaftszentrums Zürich entwickelt. Entlang der wirtschaftlichen Kraftlinie von Zürich über Oerlikon zum Flughafen Kloten wächst hier die dynamischste Region der Schweiz als bandartige Agglomeration. Mit Inbetriebnahme der ersten Etappe der Glattalbahn im Jahr 2005 erhielt diese neue »Glattalstadt« eine Art Rückgrat.

e

large-scale halls of the Zurich trade fair, which is surrounded by car dealers and small-scale residential housing. Furthermore, clusters of service companies have emerged along the so-called Glattalbahn, the rapid transit rail system that follows the course of Thurgauer Strasse. The private design plan for the area stipulates a permissible usage ratio of 420 per cent.

Support Structure

The buildings are based by means of cased foundation piles on a layer of molasse sedimentary rock, which was found on the site at a depth of eighteen to twenty-eight metres, under artificial backfilling, lake sediments, and moraine. In the areas where the basements were not built over [the square], they serve as tension piles against upwelling. This was necessary, as measurements of groundwater levels showed that the upper, free groundwater level is only 1.2 metres underground.

The line of the Glatt-Stollen sewage tunnel transects the site diagonally, at a depth of around fourteen metres. It is a pipe with a diameter of around five metres, which could not be intersected. The piles had to be bored five metres from the tunnel axis. A 1.4- to 1.8-metre-thick, pre-stressed base plate was necessary to absorb the support loads over the Glatt-Stollen. The base plate had to be constructed in three-metre-thick segments to ensure sufficient counterweight against the upwelling.

In order to achieve the greatest possible usage flexibility, the shell construction of the four towers and the bases was built as a skeleton structure, with an extensive support grid. The ceilings are suspended freely from the core to the façade, and are twenty-six to twenty-eight centimetres thick. They were partially made as pre-stressed, cast-in-place concrete ceilings, because this was the only way to meet the following challenging requirements: low construction height [this enabled the realization of an additional floor in the case of the ninety-metre tower], reduction of the net weight, fire safety, and feasibility of the thermo active building system.

The seismic design was carried out using the response spectrum method. Its dynamic calculation takes into account the fundamental oscillation, as well as the significant higher forms of natural oscillation. The core walls stabilize the high-rise towers. As the core is very narrow in relation to the height of the ninety- and seventy-metre towers, two concrete walls were built in each – from the core to the façade supports, on the seventeenth and eighteenth floors – for stabilization purposes. The core walls are forty centimetres thick and were made of B 45/35 concrete. The maximum wind displacement of the eighty-eight-metre tower is forty-four millimetres, according to calculations.

Bicycle Parking

The 141 bicycle parking spaces in the underground garage are accessed via a cycle ramp by the rail embankment on Andreasstrasse. This part of the garage has its own emergency exit staircases.

Zurich-Nord

Leutschenbach is one of the largest development areas in the city of Zurich. The former industrial estate in Zurich-Nord encompasses an area of around sixty hectares. Based on the first project studies regarding the high-rise ensemble, in 1998 the city launched a cooperative development plan for Leutschenbach, together with the private landowners. The development principles that were set out formed the basis for the current building and zoning regulations. Owing to its location, Zurich-Nord has developed into a strategically relevant district within the Swiss financial and commercial centre of Zurich. The most dynamic Swiss region is developing as a ribbon-like agglomeration along the economic axis of power from Zurich, via Oerlikon to the Kloten Airport. When the first stretch of the Glattalbahn rapid transit rail system was put into operation in 2005, it formed a type of backbone for this new »Glattal town«.

Das Tragwerk in der Bauphase
The support structure during construction

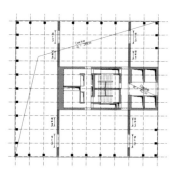

**Statisches System des Doppelturms:
Aussteifender Kern mit Outrigger**
Structural system of the double tower:
fortified core with outrigger

Wir danken allen Bildrechteinhabern für die Erlaubnis zum Abdruck in dieser Publikation. Trotz intensiver Bemühungen konnten evtl. bis Redaktionsschluss nicht alle Bildrechteinhaber ausfindig gemacht werden. Zur Klärung eventueller Ansprüche bitten wir, sich ggf. mit den Herausgebern in Verbindung zu setzen.
The editors would like to thank all image rights holders who have kindly given their permission for publication. Every effort has been made to identify all rights holders before publication. We would ask any rights holders we did not manage to contact to get in touch with the editors.

Stefan Müller I Berlin
04, 07, 09, 10, 12, 14, 20, 22, 24, 26, 28 unten/bottom, 29 unten/bottom, 30 unten/bottom, 31 unten/bottom, 33, 43, 44, 46, 48, 50 unten/bottom, 51 unten/bottom, 52 unten/bottom, 53 unten/bottom, 54, 62, 64, 66, 75 unten/bottom, 78 Mitte + unten/middle + bottom

Implenia Schweiz AG
08, 77, 78

ETH-Bibliothek Zürich/Zurich, Bildarchiv/Stiftung Luftbild Schweiz
16

Olivia Heussler I Zürich/Zurich
17, 19, 28 oben/top, 29 oben/top, 30 oben/top, 31 oben/top
42, 58, 59

Birkhäuser Verlag Basel
18

UAA Ungers Archiv für Architekturwissenschaft
21 oben/top, Mitte/middle

Wikimedia Foundation Inc.
21 unten/bottom, 37 unten/bottom

Architectural Review, Bd. 124/Vol. 124, 1923
34, 35

Carol Herselle Krinsky, Rockefeller Center, New York 1978
36, 37 oben/top

Stadtbaukunst alter und neuer Zeit, Bd. 1/Vol.1, 1920
38

Paola Chiarella
39

Peter Noever [Hg./Ed.], Tyrannei des Schönen. Architektur der Stalin-Zeit, München/Munich 1994
40

Arbeitsgemeinschaft atelier ww Max Dudler
55 oben + unten/top + bottom, 56, 57, 60, 68, 69, 70, 71, 72, 73, 76
50 oben/top, 51 oben/top, 52 oben/top, 53 oben/top

Senatsverwaltung für Stadtentwicklung und Umwelt, Berlin
61

atelier ww Architekten SIA AG
74 oben/top

Gruenberg & Partner AG, Zürich/Zurich
74 unten/bottom

Stäger & Nägeli AG, Zürich/Zurich
75 oben/top

Hochbauamt Stadt Zürich/Zurich
77 oben/top

Max Dudler
77 unten/bottom

Henauer Gugler AG, Zürich/Zurich
79

Dieses Buch wurde unterstützt durch:
This book was funded by:

Axa Leben AG, Zürich / Implenia Schweiz AG, Dietikon / Aepli Metallbau AG, Gossau / Anliker AG, Emmenbrücke / Bardak AG, Zürich / Elevator Consulting GmbH, Gettnau / Emch Aufzüge AG, Bern / Fahrni Fassadensysteme AG, Lyss / Félix Constructions SA, Denges / FSB- Beschläge, Brakel (Deutschland) / Hofmann Naturstein GmbH & Co. KG, Würzburg (Deutschland) / Mäder Bauphysik, Winterthur / RJM Consulting Feuerweheinsatzplanung, Winkel / Soprema AG, Spreitenbach / Ernst Schweizer AG, Metallbau